CARSON KRESSLEY

with *Riann Smith*

A CHEEKY Guide to feeling sexier in Your OWN skin and UNLEASHING Your Personal Style

St. Martin's Griffin
New York

Intro p. viii, photo courtesy of Getty Images; p. 2, photo courtesy of Carson Kressley; p. 3, photo courtesy of Carson Kressley; p. 4, photo courtesy of Matt Albiani; p. 5, photo courtesy of Getty Images; p. 8, photos courtesy of Carson Kressley; p. 28, photo courtesy of Getty Images; p. 57, photo courtesy of Getty Images; p. 68, photo courtesy of Matt Albiani; p. 88, photo courtesy of the Ogunquit Playhouse; p. 95, photo courtesy of Getty Images; p. 110, photo courtesy of Carson Kressley; p. 111, photo courtesy of Carson Kressley; p. 114, photo courtesy of Lisa Quiñones Photography; p. 117, photo courtesy of Anansa Sims; p. 120, photo courtesy of Heather Thomson; p. 128, photo courtesy of Ashley Loewen; p. 132, photo courtesy of Ginger Zee; p. 135, photo courtesy of Carson Kressley; p. 140, photo courtesy of Getty Images; p. 144, photo courtesy of Carson Kressley; p. 149, photo courtesy of Carson Kressley; p. 155, photo courtesy of Carson Kressley; p. 158, photo courtesy of Carson Kressley; p. 161, photo courtesy of QVC Inc., copyright © QVC, Inc.; p. 166, photo courtesy of Carson Kressley; p. 167, photo courtesy of Carson Kressley; p. 168, photo courtesy of Carson Kressley; p. 169, photo courtesy of Getty Images; p. 171, photo courtesy of Carson Kressley; p. 173, photo courtesy of Alysia Reiner; p. 174, photo courtesy of Carson Kressley; p. 176, photo courtesy of Carson Kressley; p. 177, photo courtesy of Vivica A. Fox; p. 178, photo courtesy of Carson Kressley; p. 179, photo courtesy of Logo TV; p. 181, photo courtesy of Matt Albiani; p. 182, photo courtesy of Matt Albiani; p. 183, photo courtesy of Carson Kressley

Printed in the United States of America. For information, address St. Martin's Press, 175 Fifth Avenue, New York, N.Y. 10010.

www.stmartins.com

BOOK DESIGN BY SHUBHANI SARKAR
sarkardesignstudio.com

The Library of Congress Cataloging-in-Publication Data is available upon request.

ISBN 978-1-250-08558-0
(paper over board)

ISBN 978-1-250-08559-7 (e-book)

Our books may be purchased in bulk for promotional, educational, or business use. Please contact your local bookseller or the Macmillan Corporate and Premium Sales Department at 1-800-221-7945, extension 5442, or by e-mail at MacmillanSpecialMarkets@macmillan.com.

First Edition: October 2016

10 9 8 7 6 5 4 3 2 1

To mom, and every style-seeking woman in the universe,
who lives large, loves herself hard, and *tszuj* wants to be fabulous

CONTENTS

Omigod! You Look Amazing! 1

1. MAKEOVERS, MAKEUNDERS & TAKING CARE OF *MOI* 7

2. OUT WITH THE OLD . . . IN WITH THE *OOH!* 27

3. I JUST LOVE A WOMAN IN UNIFORM 45

4. BEING A BARGAINISTA 67

5. WHO, WHAT, *WEAR* 87

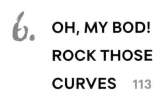

6. OH, MY BOD! ROCK THOSE CURVES 113

7. REALLY, I WOKE UP LIKE THIS! 139

8. JUST BETWEEN US GALS 165

Acknowledgments 183

Me with shoppers at a personal style event I hosted
at the New York & Company boutique in Los Cerritos,
California. Looking good, girls!

OMIGOD!
You Look Amazing!

Hi LADIES! IT'S BEEN A LONG TIME . . . too long! How the heck *are* you? Well, I finally dusted off my laptop (I was using it as a chic little breakfast-in-bed tray) and birthed this insanely witty style tome, just for you. Like other timeless classics, from *War and Peace* to *Fifty Shades of Grey*, it promises to be an absolute page-turner. Consume it à la carte (hold the dressing!) or gobble it up in toto. Because, Toto, we're not in Kansas anymore! Or maybe we are? I happen to adore Kansas!

Here's the real reason why I wrote this book: I genuinely want to know if you think it makes my gluteus look maximus. Okay, I'm just jerking your chain belt; maybe that's not the only reason. See, there's this little thing that happens to me just about every day of my life, everywhere I go—from L.A. to N.Y. and every small town in between. Women stop me on the street, asking for fashion advice or begging me to make them over. Sometimes they just want a hug. (God, can you imagine how lucky I'd be if I wasn't gay? *Bow chicka wow wow . . .)* This phenomenon actually started much earlier than you'd think, when I styled my big sister for prom night. I felt a deep sense of pride for my aesthetic sensibilities: Sis might not have been named prom queen or gotten lucky without my help! To this day, I love spending every waking minute making people look and feel better. I can't help myself. And I want to do it with you, right here, right now. Can you pencil me in? You better.

With decades under my Hermès belt working with high-profile clients all over the world, styling for top companies like Ralph Lauren to Neiman Marcus to Macy's, starring in and hosting countless TV and award shows, winning an Emmy, writing a best-selling men's style book and a pretty darn fabulous children's book, spending time with God (Oprah), and designing my own fashion line—I knew it was high time I shined some positivity on the complex cocktail of women and that ever-elusive idea, personal style. But here's what: Lately, I've noticed things have been starting to get a little, well, *stressy*. Never before have we been bombarded with so much pressure to look better, dress better, shop better, Instagram our toenail art better. From flash sales to department-store doorbusters, from celebrity blogs to boob jobs on reality TV, the modern world is a virtual self-betterment bonanza. And the more choices we have, the more daunting the process becomes. I started asking myself, in this

I've been lucky to do zillions of makeovers on Oprah's show and network.
O is the real deal, and she loves to laugh. She also smells like Santa Barbara lavender.

sea of style confusion, are women even having *fun* anymore?

Like the question of whether extraterrestrials are among us or if Invisalign has truly lined up Tom Cruise's incisors to perfection, I think the answer is "not sure." I've worked with thousands of women from coast to coast, though, and I know a few things for certain. Whether you live in Pacoima, Tacoma, or Tallahassee, you want to feel beautiful, confident, and sexy but don't know where to start. Sometimes you feel frustrated by fashion and can't figure out which trends to follow and which to flee . . . so you don't bother at all. Between your family, your job, and your other commitments, you don't have the time, money, or inspiration to totally transform your look. And when it comes to how most of you feel about your bodies, you have more baggage than Air Japan's international check-in counter. Someone pass me a Xany!

I know it's safer to sit back and say you're too tired, you're too busy, you're too broke, you're too fat, you're too skinny, you're too married, you're too single, you're too this or too that to even care about evolving your style. Plus, it's easy to let all the people and priorities in your life stand between you and your best self. Your kids, your boss, your beau, your Labradoodle—all of them tend to get put first, which gives you a perfect excuse to do nothing. And even when you want to do something nice for yourself, from a blowout to a mani-pedi to browsing shoe porn online, a nagging voice sets in: *Should I really be using this time for me? Isn't there something more important I need to do, like finish my kid's science fair project or reprogram our universal remote?*

Let's couch-surf ourselves back in time together, back to that fabulous old L'Oréal tagline: "Because you're worth it." Remember how confident that voice sounded? Do *you* treat yourself like you're worth it? It sounds so simple, yet so few women really follow that mantra when it comes to themselves. But here's the honest-to-mod truth: If you don't prioritize yourself in terms of grooming and style, you're not going to harness that powerful version of you, the woman capable of running the show at work, in your family, and in your community. And then everything will go south, sweetie, and we're not just talking about your derriere. The motto I live by is, "All the world's a stage; make sure you have the right costume," and that's much of what this book is about—finding it, claiming it, feeling your best self in it.

For me, that meant wearing a plaid polyester leisure suit to my first day of kindergarten. What's your personal statement going to be? How do you want to reinvent yourself? I'm not expecting you to know the answers yet. Sometimes all you need is a best friend (or zany blond fairy godstylist) to come in and say, "Hey, let's figure this out together and have as much fun doing it as possible." Or, to shoplift one of my favorite Pinterest quotes, "Life's too short. Buy the shoes." Just think of how boring Imelda Marcos or Carrie Bradshaw would be if they were sensible!

It's high time we start having fun again and enjoying clothes and the skin we're in. It's either

I'm also wearing silk paisley Underoos.

that or a mini-lobotomy, people! Oh, that's right, I don't have health insurance *anyway*! Kidding aside, I want you to know that being a fierce fashionista is just not that difficult. Along with the right tools, tips, and tricks, you have the power to transform your style and self-perception this second, just by shifting your mind-set from woe-is-me to wow-is-me. You picked up this book (by the way, did I say thank you? Thank you!) because you wanted to take action, to kick your entire look and your life up a notch. So what are we waiting for . . . besides a 99-percent-off Manolo sale?

Once you commit to some positive changes and decide you're actually going to have a good time with it (you'll get divalicious tips from a famous drag queen, but our mission should never be a

be homework, dollars, and deep thoughts involved, too (like, should I get Princess Kate bangs . . . for my dog?), but how much of an investment you make is up to you. All you need is an open mind, a game plan, and some trusted resources in your orbit. And as sure as Sofía Vergara's cleavage makes an awesome taco holder, I'm going to help you get there.

So, repeat after *moi* . . .

- **Can I feel happier about my looks? (Yes!)**
- **Can I fearlessly transform myself? (Yes!)**
- **Can I enjoy getting dressed every morning? (Yes!)**
- **Can I have more fun with fashion? (Yes!)**
- **Can I feel more "put together" at special events? (Yes!)**
- **Can I love my body, no matter what? (Yes!)**
- **Can I take better care of myself? (Yes!)**
- **Can I take Bradley Cooper to the Golden Globes? (Get in line!)**

drag), the rest is easy-peasy-lemon-squeezie. You'll be learning oh-so-doable techniques for upgrading your look and streamlining a confusing closet. You'll discover unexpected ways to shop and resources that are right under your nose . . . or on your smartphone. You'll find solutions for occasion-specific dressing, playing up your *ass*-ets, and cultivating affordable style gurus. You'll hear how to use hairspray to keep your underwear from getting stuck to a formal gown (learned that one at the Miss Universe Pageant—thank you, Miss Trinidad and Tobago!). And you'll get tons of insider style secrets I've picked up from some of my favorite women on the planet. *Psst* . . . some of them are Oscar winners!

But before we get ahead of ourselves, it's key to remember my favorite T-shirt slogan: BEYONCÉ WASN'T BUILT IN A DAY. Looking fierce takes commitment, creativity, and swagger. There will

Did you say all of this aloud to yourself, three times fast for bonus points? Fantastic! It's the first baby step toward becoming a more fabulous you. Because you and your personal emoji can live a fashionable life if you just have the right mind-set—and that work-it-girl confidence will spill over into every other aspect of your life. Since you've acknowledged that the biggest thing holding you back has been nothing more than an attitude glitch, taking off is a snap. So, let's launch! I'm helping you GPS your inner glamazon, and we've got a lot of ground to cover. There's no room for haters on this journey—unless you hate rules, like I do. Shall we "tszuj" do it?

Ladies, if I can jump through hoops for fashion, so can you!

before

after

makeovers, MAKEUNDERS & TAKING CARE of MOI

MY SERENITY PRAYER

Beauty gods, grant me the serenity
to accept the features I cannot change,
the courage to self-tan the things I can,
and the wisdom to know the difference...
between Botox and filler.

AS FAR BACK AS I CAN REMEMBER, I've been making myself over. (What, did you think I was born with this Don Johnson mane and pillowy lips? Oh, wait, I was . . . sort of!) But my metamorphosis from country bumpkin to haute couture wasn't all roses and rosé. In fact, it bordered on IKEA-furniture-assembly-instructions confusing. Brace yourself, dear reader, because my style journey began with none other than life's most marketable phallic symbol: lipstick. Freud would've had a field day with me . . . on his Barcalounger!

It all started when I was a young Tater Tot living in Claussville, a small town in Pennsylvania Dutch country. It was the 1970s, the Watergate scandal was in full swing, and hot pants were all the rage. But not in my sheltered neighborhood, silly; people were too busy churning butter! Still, Mom would get Avon deliveries (Ding-dong! Avon calling!), which at the time was the closest I could get to the glamour of the beauty-and-fashion industry. Most boys my age cared about *Battlestar Galactica* and baseball cards, but for me, seeing that new Avon delivery at the door was like Christmas in July! I'll never forget the shiny

Hanging with my mom, Barbara, in our kitchen (of course it had carpet, it was the seventies!). Mom was the first one to plant the seed that clothes matter.

Riding "Unchaperoned," my Saddlebred, at the World's Championship Horse Show in 2011. I saved up to buy my first horse at sixteen. Chicer than a Honda Civic!

turquoise plastic box that housed forty mini-lipsticks with yummy, exotic names like Crystal Red, Caramel Candy, and Coral Kiss. After I'd arrive home from elementary school, while Mom was still working, I'd go through her lipsticks, trying out each one in the mirror, practicing my pucker and pout. Afterward, I'd carefully resculpt each angled lipstick edge with a butter knife to hide any signs of use (like I still do when I raid medicine cabinets at housewarming parties).

Since my mother had won the title of Miss Pennsylvania Milk-maid—Mom sure was a fox—she had a crown in her closet and a fabulous chiffon dress and dyed-to-match sparkly shoes. With my lips glossed in Rum Raisin, I couldn't resist trying on her clothes and jewels. It was like my own secret fashion show; all I needed was a hit

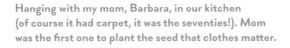

Always be a first-rate version of yourself, instead of a second-rate version of somebody else.

JUDY GARLAND

song from the Carpenters in the background and a slow dance with David Cassidy. No one in my family ever said anything, but I think they knew what was up. I felt ashamed. It wasn't until I fell in love with seventies television drama queens that I realized how empowering fashion could be. Rhoda rocked a Boho headscarf before any of us knew what Boho was; Jennifer Hart sizzled in her glam St. John pantsuits; Carol Brady's mullet was pure trendsetting magic; and Endora and Mrs. Roper swung their colorful caftans around in Pucci perfection. "More," I said, "more!"

Add that to my growing experience competing on the equestrian circuit, where I saw the international set donning ultrachic ensembles, from horsey Hermès scarves and bangles to Bianca Jagger hats and Jackie O sunglasses. I started to realize that, wow, there's a big, exciting world of style out there, and one day I'm going to not just live in that world, but help women around the world get the keys to the fashion kingdom! In case you're wondering, I pictured that kingdom looking like a cross between Churchill Downs and Studio 54.

But my dreams of disco balls and world fashion domination would have to wait. Meanwhile, I had to worry about getting hung on lockers at school and beaten up at the mall, when all I wanted to do was wear my Coca-Cola rugby shirt and Swatch watch and window-shop for Mackenzie Phillips, my dream makeover client, in peace. Cue the violin music and pass me an orange Fanta! I was an after-school special in the making.

And since it's just us girlfriends, I'm going to tell you another deep, dark secret. I've had a nose job. A schnoz shave. A beak tweak. There, I said it. It was many seasons into *Queer Eye*, and it was a splurge on myself that I could finally afford. I had always been self-conscious about the way my nose hooked down. So I went to a plastic surgeon to the stars in New York City and said I needed a little nip-tuck, nothing drastic. As they were putting me under anesthesia, I freaked out, wondering, *Can I really go through with this?*

When I woke up after surgery, I kid you not, the first thing I saw on television was myself in an NBC made-for-TV version of the classic movie, *The Year Without a Santa Claus.* John Goodman was Santa, and I played, of course, an elf. My first thought was, *Is this a dream?* and my second was, *Wait, do I still have my old nose?* Once the bandages came off, I did an unveiling of my newly tapered *naso* to my friends at my apartment a week later, after I had properly liquored them up. Most of them didn't care or really didn't notice the difference. But I did, and I carried myself differently because of it. New nostrils, new attitude!

We've all had our moments of reshaping and reinventing ourselves in hopes that somehow it will all click into place and we will finally look in the mirror and say, "Hello, gorgeous." I don't know what your own hot-button issues are, but I know what it feels like to not feel comfortable in my own skin and to have the motivation and itch to want to change it. My feeling is you can sit around and complain about something; learn to accept it (like I accept my freakishly skinny arms—in the gay world, being buff is a big deal) or decide to take action like you're Shailene Woodley confronting your inner demons.

It may not amount to a drastic move like plastic surgery (which by the way, I don't casually advocate), but a li'l refining can go a long way.

- -

Tszuj Do It... Book yourself an impromptu pampering appointment, like a deluxe paraffin mani-pedi or a blowout . . . but it's an exploding offer that ends today! (I used my Crazy Eddie voice for this one. Sorry, you have to buy the audiobook to hear how awesome it sounds, or be a child of the seventies with access to N.Y.C. cable stations.)

- -

QUIZ: ARE YOU READY TO UPGRADE YOUR LOOK?

1. Congratulations, you just won a free hair makeover from the best salon in town. You:

    a. Are gung-ho to change your color, cut, or style. Snip it, whip it, flip it!

    b. Defer to their suggestions but tell them you don't want to do anything too trendy.

    c. Get a consult first, but wind up with something similar to your usual trim.

2. You have a $100 gift certificate to Sephora. You:

    a. Get a full-face makeover plus lashes for an upcoming party.

    b. Buy a trio of lipsticks: two tried and true and one wild card.

    c. Forget it's in your wallet or use it on your niece for Christmas.

3. In the waiting room of your dermatologist's office, you see before and after pics of a certain nonsurgical product/procedure you haven't tried but are intrigued by. You think:

    a. Wow. I'll ask my doc about it today. Maybe I'll give myself an early birthday gift.

    b. I'll take some brochures home and mull it over before my next appointment.

    c. Too risky, too pricey. What if it backfires and I wind up on Botched?

4. Have you whitened your teeth, gotten a spray tan, a blowout, facial, or tried shellac or gel nails recently?

    a. You do all of the above regularly, plus lasers, plumpers, highlights, and more.

    b. You've done many of these things but never as often as you would like.

    c. You get your nails and hair done before a trip or a holiday event, and that's it.

5. Your friend looks so much better after doing a cosmetic procedure. You:

    a. Ask for her doctor's name pronto—you're going to look just as fabulous!

    b. Feel nudged to think about any improvements you've put on the back burner.

    c. Are secretly a tad jealous that she splurged on herself, but you tell yourself she looks fake.

MOSTLY A'S: *The Chameleon*

You're always game for transformation. You take pride in updating your appearance and almost feel competitive about keeping up with the latest procedures and trends to stay young and fresh. Just don't get on the makeover roller coaster, because more isn't always more. See my Barbie story at the end of this chapter.

MOSTLY B'S: *The Evolver*

You know it's key to update numero uno, but sometimes you wind up on the fence. As long as the expert is well qualified and you've done all your homework on the pros and cons, carve out the time to do one nonsurgical improvement in the next month that you know will give you a little boost, like a facial peel or tooth whitening.

MOSTLY C'S: *The Evergreen*

You can't help seeing the downside to most upgrades, partly because you haven't done your research and partly because you're scared that change equals a frivolous mistake in the making. Next time someone asks you what you want for a gift, say you'd love a gift card to a medi-spa or salon. Use it as a chance to experiment on a small scale.

carson confession: MY FIRST ENCOUNTER WITH BEAVER

I did a show for the Oprah Winfrey Network called *Carson Nation*, where we traveled around the United States in an Airstream trailer full of style. We specifically went to small towns where people traditionally didn't have access to the latest trends. Which brings me to my trip to Beaver, Utah. My subject was Jane, a tall, beautiful, fifty-five-year-old mother in a Mormon family who had lost an adult daughter to cancer. For the past year, Jane didn't bother getting her hair done or wearing makeup. The pain, anguish, and grief overwhelmed her, and she just stopped living. Going through something so traumatic made everything else, especially her looks, seem unimportant.

It was our mission to get Jane back in the groove. We launched a crash course in "me time." We went through her closet together and realized how many terrific pieces she already owned. A shopping trip got her into some new clothes and introduced more color into her wardrobe—which was key to lifting her spirits.

Then we colored her hair an amazing auburn tone, which set off her bright blue eyes. Believe it or not, little things like getting her hair and nails done snapped her back into living in the most sensory kind of way. When we left the salon she ran her fingers through her hair and said, "This looks good, this feels good; I feel more alive."

Cut to a fantastic family reunion. Remember, she was Mormon, so we're talking a *lot* of relatives—truly a stadium of superfans. Jane was glowing, and it wasn't just her spray tan. Everyone was so proud of her and dazzled by her new look that it brought people to tears. It was clear that she was back in the fold and was ready to be a fully present wife, grandmother, and mother to her four children again. It was in that moment of realization that Jane acknowledged that her daughter wouldn't want her to be living like she had been, and the best way to honor her memory was to continue taking good care of herself.

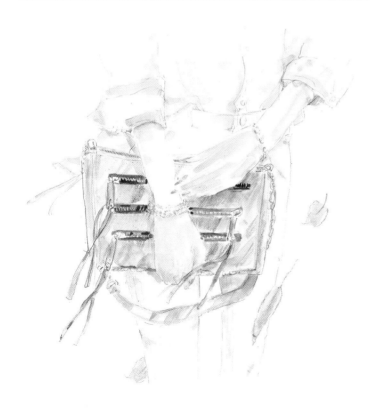

FIVE UPGRADES
THAT MAKE EVERYONE LOOK *amazeballs*

There are a few universal beauty boosters that tend to look good on anyone, anywhere, anytime. Try just one and you'll find it hard not to fawn over yourself.

1. A FAUX GLOW

I feel naked without a tan (and look best naked with one!). It's insurance that even if I've put on a few pounds or my skin looks like gray Play-Doh, I still have a sun-kissed aura.

Face Tanner:
My fave drugstore product is Jergens Natural Glow FACE Daily Facial Moisturizer with Sunscreen in Fair to Medium (they also make Medium to Dark for deeper skin tones). It gradually builds, so you don't get an Oompa Loompa effect. Blend into your neck and hairline (ears too) for a seamless look, then apply your regular makeup. With your new base tan, you may only need concealer.

- -

BUTT *seriously* . . .
Soak a cotton ball with facial astringent and rub to remove stubborn self-tanner streaks. Still there? Try a dot of diluted nail polish remover.

- -

Body Tanner: When I travel, I pack Tan Towels, which are so easy to rub anywhere for a pseudo–vitamin D boost (tantowel.com). Clarins makes a Self Tanning Instant Gel that dries superfast and doesn't have that icky smell (clarinsusa.com). If you have a brand that you already love, make your supply last longer *and* achieve a more natural look by swirling it with a dab of moisturizer. After washing hands, rub a dry washcloth over knuckles, knees, elbows, and ankles, where color can be a stage-five clinger.

Spray Tan: When I arrived on the set of *Dancing with the Stars*, I noticed everyone walking around half naked in black towels. Had I joined a cult? Then I caught on: They had spray tans that were staining everything. Orange really *is* the new black! Follow suit and wear dark, breathable cotton to the salon. If you're a newbie, try the lightest mist first. You want to look sun-kissed, not like you were dipped in carrot ginger dressing. Is it gross that I'm getting hungry?

- -

BUTT *seriously* . . .
Try Quick Tan Instant Bronzing Spray by Body Drench (sallybeauty.com). Have a friend spray you head to toe, preferably outside or in the shower. Better yet, make it someone else's shower, because when you're done, the place will look like graffiti art gone wrong. But *you'll* look amazing.

- -

Bronzer: If you tend to break out after applying self-tanners and spray tans to your face, bronzing powder is a fab alternative. There are so many brands out there, but my standouts are Guerlain Terracotta Bronzing Powder and, for oil-free fans, Tarte Amazonian Clay Waterproof Bronzer (both available at beauty.com). Lightly swipe it across your nose, from cheek to cheek. This is where the sun actually hits your face, along with your forehead and chin. Be prepared for "So, how was Hawaii?"

Tszuj Do It... As a young fashion stylist working on sets around the world, I would hear a legend that Kate Moss used vodka and lemon juice to keep her blond highlights looking fierce. Try it! You're golden . . . and so is your hair! Now that's what I call a vodka tonic.

2. HOT DAMN! HAIR

Blowout: Who doesn't look more put together with a professional blow-dry? Now that there are so many blow-dry bars around, it's easy to book one right after work so you look great for an evening event. If you can't get there, I love the John Frieda Salon Shape 1.5-inch Hot Air Brush. It's under $30 and will give you bounce and smoothness at home (amazon.com).

Conditioning Treatment: If you can book a fast conditioning treatment before your blow-dry, even better, especially if you color your hair regularly and suffer from dry ends and dullness. Your hair feels cleaner, fuller, and shinier, especially for those with lifeless or frizzy manes. At home, I love a yummy coconut hair mask called Smooth Extender by Smooth Sexy Hair. It's reasonably priced and available at drugstores.

Highlights: No matter what shade you are, from deep brown to strawberry blond, just about everyone can benefit from a bit o' brightening around the face. Your goal is to recapture what your hair looked like as a child in summer. Mine was lemon chiffon. . . . what was yours? Stay tuned for more highlighting secrets in chapter 7.

> Twice a week, I go to a beauty salon and have my hair blown dry. It's cheaper by far than psychoanalysis, and much more uplifting.
>
> **NORA EPHRON**

3. A MEGAWATT SMILE

Ecru and cream may be in for winter coats, but not teeth. Studies show that whiter teeth make us look healthier, wealthier, and will guarantee a lifetime of fame and fortune. Okay, maybe not, but it sure feels good to go from yellow to *hello!*

Porcelain Veneers: If you have crooked, chipped, or teeny chompers and are willing to drop the cash (from $800 per tooth), this can be a serious smile changer. We've all seen this go way wrong when people go too big and too white, so keep it pearly and tasteful.

Tip: Do your uppers and lowers. No one wants to see movie-star teeth on top and rat teeth on the bottom.

Professional Whitening: If your main problem is too many espressos and liters of Barolo, but your teeth are in otherwise good condition, all you need is a good brightening. Your dentist can do in-house teeth whitening or create a mold that is used with a customized kit that works over a period of weeks. Just don't scare the pizza delivery guy when you answer the door looking like Rocky.

At-Home Whitening Kit: They can be clunky and make you drool like a mastiff, but these drugstore kits are affordable and really do make a difference. If you don't have sensitive teeth and gums, Crest Whitestrips are easiest to use and very effective. GO SMiLE's Double Action Whitening System works wonders, and its ON THE GO Teeth Whitening Pen is great for touch-ups (ulta.com). Just promise me you won't confuse it with your Clorox Bleach Pen.

4. LUSH LASHES

Nearly every celeb makes a lash-ting commitment to fill out their fringe, and that's because lashes add flirty and feminine energy to your eyes—and your entire face—like nothing else can. If you have a big event coming up, like a reunion or a wedding, use it as an excuse to try a semipermanent solution. The end result will make your heart flutter, but be warned: The upkeep may drive you batty.

Latisse: Like Miracle-Gro for your fringe! Apply the formula onto your lashes every night, making sure not to brush it elsewhere (hello, Ewok forehead). If you're diligent about applying it, expect to see results after sixteen weeks. You do have to keep it up by reapplying two to three times per week, or you'll be back to square one in less than a month. But fans will tell you it's totally worth it.

Lash Extensions: Choose from synthetic, silk, or mink lashes (minkies are feather-light but priciest). All you need is a half set, which is individually attached to your center and outer lashes, or filled in along your lash line for a more natural look. You'll need to have them redone at six to eight weeks. Have a licensed pro apply them—unless you want to star in a suburban moms' remake of *A Clockwork Orange*.

Lash Tinting: Perfect for blondes with light lashes, those with faded lash tips, and anyone looking for a little drama (who isn't?). The best part: no mascara. You can go to the beach, gym, or roll out of bed looking fab. The upkeep is a retouch every month. Consider doing a brow tint at the same time to really frame your eyes. I do both of these religiously and they work like a charm.

5. LIQUID FACE-LIFT

How *does* she look five years younger and less frowny overnight? That's what your irritated friends will be wondering. Don't tell them it's Botox and fillers! This combo will help you look more youthful and refreshed. But only have a

board-certified dermatologist perform these procedures, and beware the "beauty expert" who does Botox parties.

Botox: It doesn't fill anything, but it relaxes those pesky facial muscles so they stop working overtime between your brows (otherwise known as the "elevens"), on your forehead, your crow's feet, and even vertical neck bands, which means more smoothness and less wrinkling. Other products called Dysport and Xeomin have similar effects. Results last approximately three to six months, and even longer, depending on the product. Now for a little finger wagging: If you have any medical conditions or autoimmune disease, get the green light from your physician before being treated.

BUTT *seriously* . . .
Use arnica to keep swelling at bay after your injections (wholefoodsmarket.com). If you're looking bruisey and don't want to frighten small children, lightly dab on concealers by Dermablend (beauty.com).

> I'm not saying that putting on makeup will change the world or even your life, but it can be a first step in learning things about yourself you may never have discovered otherwise.

KEVYN AUCOIN

Fillers: Fillers like Juvéderm and Restylane are ideal for areas where you've had fat and bone loss, like your temples, cheeks, jawline, and around the lips. Restylane can also gently erase a sunken look if you have deep-set eyes with hollows emerging underneath, as can another smooth gel product like Belotero. They are made with hyaluronic acid, which sounds like a scary club kid drug but is actually a naturally occurring substance our bodies already make (it may also stimulate collagen production!). Results last from six months to up to two years, depending on the product. If you need a correction, effects can be reversed with hyaluronic acid-based fillers but may not with other dermal fillers, so ask first. When it comes to fillers, less is more. Start with just a drop and have your doctor add more later if you feel you need it.

- -

Tszuj Do It... Download the Plastic Surgery Simulator on iTunes for a fun-house-mirror thrill. Do it with friends' faces! See, it could totally be worse!

- -

carson confession:

- - - - - - - - - - - - - - - - - - -

I CAN'T FEEL MY FACE WHEN I'M WITH YOU . . .

- - - - - - - - - - - - - - - - - - -

Remember how I told you that I have naturally pillowy lips? The upper one is courtesy of my big brother, who put me on a seesaw "so we could play a little game" and then got off without telling me. That was painful on so many levels. Anyway, while I was working on *Queer Eye*, we scored an invite to see a top cosmetic dermatologist in Manhattan for free. ("Sign me up," I chanted!) Instead of asking the doc what would look most natural, I told him right away that I wanted my lower lip to match my upper one. So he did what I asked. When I walked out of the office into the waiting room, Thom and Jai flipped. "Carson, your face is bleeding!" they cried, too freaked out to get a procedure themselves. "But it's *fwee!*" I snapped back, holding an ice pack to my mouth. All I remember is my lower lip feeling like there were little metal BBs in it.

After my appointment, I followed my doctor's orders to "smile, frown, smile, frown" for an hour to evenly distribute the product. Walking down Park Avenue, I looked a little like a victim of tardive dyskinesia, ready for my class-action lawsuit. Eventually, it settled in and all looked good, though in hindsight, I wouldn't have insisted on doing my lower lip. I learned that day to ask for the doctor's opinion before assuming I knew what was best. I also learned not to bring friends with me to the dermatologist. Still, I'm such a fan of injectables that I might as well have bumper stickers that say I BREAK FOR BOTOX and FILL 'ER UP! because in small doses, they make me look more rested and refreshed.

CHEAP 'N' CHIC tweaks

Whether you're still saving up to have a brand-new-you procedure or just can't justify the price tag of one, don't think that self-improvement is an all-or-nothing game. These boosters are the next best thing:

INSTEAD OF . . . LIP INJECTIONS

Try . . . Dior Addict Lip Maximizer. Two weeks to a plumper pout, no needles necessary. The pale pink gloss looks pretty on its own, too (available at most major department stores).

INSTEAD OF . . . PORCELAIN VENEERS

Try . . . Supersmile Professional Whitening System toothpaste plus rosy-red lipstick with a bluish (never orange) undertone that makes your teeth look brighter by contrast (walmart.com).

INSTEAD OF . . . HAIR EXTENSIONS

Try . . . SHE USA hair extensions. These clip-ins are made with real hair with keratin tips in systems that actually look legit. Instead of doing the real deal, which can be expensive and damaging to hair, these are good training wheels. Just don't get them caught in your Cuisinart (socapusa.com).

INSTEAD OF . . . LASH EXTENSIONS

Try . . . Ardell Individual Duralash Flare Mini Black lashes. Apply these natural-looking individual falsies starting at the middle of your lash line and work your way outward. Tip: Use dark glue; white spots look so obvi (amazon.com).

INSTEAD OF . . . RHINOPLASTY

Try . . . contouring powder, like Kevyn Aucoin The Sculpting Powder. Swipe either side of your nose using an angled brush. Add a highlighting powder, like MAC Shaping Powder in Off White with Fine Pearl down your bridge . . . then blur those lines, baby (both at sephora.com).

addictive MAKEOVER apps

Now that you have the glamazon basics, it's time to go wild and start playing. You know that creepy word "experimentation," which your guidance counselor used in high school? Well, this form of experimentation is the best kind, because it's herpes- and hangover-free! (Sorry . . . TMI?)

modiface.com

It's the gold standard of virtual makeovers, with apps for your face, eyes, lips, nails, hair, and skin. Upload a photo of yourself from your computer, Facebook, or via your ModiFace account. (You have the option of uploading a model instead, but where's the enlightenment in that?) Once your mug is up on the screen, start exploring. Mink shadow! How to find your skin tone and undertone! It's a playground for color junkies and indirectly gives you a tutorial on what combos really work for you. It sources tons of cosmetic brands, so when you find a product you like, you'll actually know what to buy. Oh, and their ModiFace Mirror app is killer. Imagine digitally applying lip, eye, and foundations in real time on your iPad screen (or at Sephora), just by tapping from a color wheel.

- - - - - - - - - - - - - - - - - - - -

BUTT seriously . . .

You may think of Toppík as a Hair Club for Men thingy, but their Hair Fattener seriously improves texture and fullness in female hair, along with their Hair Building Fiber powder (toppik.com). I need this product like I need oxygen, sweet potato fries, and *Bravo*.

- - - - - - - - - - - - - - - - - - - -

taaz.com

I adore this site, along with their Hair Try On app for my iPhone and iPad. Upload a photo of yourself with your hair off your face, and if it's long enough, pull it back in a pony. Demo tons of colors and styles—it's totally entertaining (I personally look fierce with Edie Falco's windswept crop). See how your skin tone lightens or darkens with different hair colors and how your face shape changes with different lengths. Not only can you do hair demos and spend quality space-out time browsing through galleries, you'll get beauty how-tos based on the looks of the moment. Plus, you can ask their experts questions like "What hair works best for a wedding . . . so I can outshine the bride?"

dailymakeover.com

Part of transforming your look is having a clue about what you want to feel like all dolled up—think holiday parties, birthday bashes, and date nights. What better way to find out than to attend a virtual event where you're the star? I've been to enough award shows to know a smoking-hot look when I see one. Now it's your turn to see what looks smoking hot on you. This site has a clever one-click system where you can virtually try on the exact hair, makeup, and jewelry looks from celebs in galleries like Red Carpet Glamour. Who's queen of the runway now . . . besides me?

carson confession: MY CREAM TURNED INTO A NIGHTMARE!

One of the fun things I get to do is go to gifting suites for award shows like the Emmys or the Oscars—basically, mobile makeover studios packed into hotel rooms. Everyone is pushing their wares and getting photos of you trying their products. There was an amazing new unisex face cream that claimed to freeze your wrinkles and fill in the fine lines with silicone. It was thick and had the consistency of Noxema. I rubbed some onto the top of my hand and fell in love. All the fine lines were filled in, and my skin was as smooth as the Bieb's chest.

Weeks later, I decided to try it on my face. I put a nice layer of the cream under my eyes before a black-tie event. It worked like a charm—as if I'd spackled my face and sanded it. I went to this sit-down dinner in my wrinkle-free tux with my wrinkle-free face, feeling fabulous. We all moved into the party room with a groovy black light, which made everything feel like a sexy discotheque. But everyone was staring at me. A friend said with widened eyes and a bit of a smirk, "Uh, Carson, you look a little scary." I ran to the bathroom, and looking back at me in the mirror was a radioactive raccoon who must have escaped Chernobyl's exclusion zone. I had giant fluorescent yellow circles around my eyes that were so freaky, I'm still not even sure it was me. I learned that night to try new products at home first.

Tszuj Do It . . . Try on a wig for the evening. Pencil in a mole. Assume a stage name. Don't leave your house . . . or do!

THE ancient LEGEND OF THE CAR SELFiE

It's Jeep Cherokee folklore that cars just have the best combo of light and shade for selfies. Why am I telling you this? Because selfies can give you a different perspective on how much your makeup is doing for you, which will help you hone your best look. Don't always look at the camera, so you can see yourself from different angles. Take some with your eyes closed and some of you laughing. Even take one upside down or at a weird angle so you're forced to see your face differently. Oh, and did I say turn off the engine first?

Now make a judgment-free first impression. What is totally working for you in this series? Be kind, as if you were looking at a friend. No, one you actually like. Look closely at your closed-eye shot. Wow, those almond eyes are gorge! Now pay attention to how your makeup is applied. Is that brown eye shadow optimizing your orbs or making them look heavy and recessed? Is it time to think about experimenting with layering colors more strategically to really bring out the shape? In your laughing shot, you might notice your lips. Why not capitalize on them by adding in a lighter gloss that really bounces light off your kisser? In one of your profile shots, you may notice that you have cheekbones that have gone totally untapped. That's prime real estate. Contour time!

The point of a makeover isn't always to fix something, but to push your best feature as far as it can possibly go. It's your choice to delete these shots, because chances are, you have better ones. These pics did their job: They gave you a different perspective that forced you to see your strengths.

BUTT seriously . . .

Everyone has a pic of themselves looking amazing. Make it your screen saver, or print it and tape it to your bathroom mirror. It's a great reminder and motivator that you totally can "go there." It doesn't have to be the same look as you have now, and in fact, it shouldn't be.

Tszuj Do It . . . Snap a selfie and upload it to the Sephora Pocket Contour Class app on your phone (m.sephora.com/pocketcontour). It will "map" your face shape, then help you apply makeup. How do you contour your face using highlighters and shadow so you appear slim 'n' sculpted? Where does the shimmer go? What to do on deeper skin tones? This app is like having a personal makeup tutor. It's almost like color by number, but with dots.

BEAUTY COUNTER
intelligence

Hey, spy girl, use your local department-store makeup counter as a beauty lab for trying on new looks. Come in with a naked face for a full treatment or a half-done face (i.e., moisturizer, primer, and foundation) if you just want specific eye, lip, or cheek techniques.

Pick Your Brand: Bobbi Brown, Laura Mercier, and Aerin are all great for natural palettes, while MAC, NARS, YSL, and Lancôme pump up the drama. If you aren't loving the finished look, try another counter or employee on another day. (If anyone raises an eyebrow at repeat visits, tell them you're an identical triplet.) Be sure to take selfies if you visit multiple counters in multiple stores, so you can compare which looks you like most.

Time It Right: The best times to hit these counters are early in the week and early in the day. In my experience, makeup artists will pay better attention to you if you make an appointment beforehand, especially if you have an event that night and want to come in before closing. Tip: Tell her

the colors of your outfit, or bring a photo in with accessories, so your look will be seamless.

Prepare to Buy: It's customary to buy your favorite product as a "thank you" for your free makeover, but don't feel compelled to shell it out for everything used (even if she gives you the stink eye). If you book a free forty-five-minute makeover or a ninety-minute consultation and makeover at Sephora, you need to buy $50 or $125 of product (respectively) after your session. The bonus of Sephora is that you're not limited to buying all one brand.

Be Savvy: Don't be afraid to shamelessly ask for free samples. I always have good luck at Nordstrom. When it comes time to buy, be selective. Products worth the investment are moisturizer, concealer, bronzer, and foundation. Meanwhile, you can "cheat and repeat" your look with similar drugstore brands of eye- and brow liner, eye shadow, mascara, and gloss. (You didn't hear it from me!)

- -

BUTT *seriously . . .*
Makeup counters harbor *mucho* bacteria, so politely push that mascara wand and lip gloss away. If you're dying to try it, swipe color on your hand only.

- -

MAKEOVER *math*

Usually addition makes my imaginary belly ring quiver, but this is just too easy!

HOW TO LOOK LIKE . . .	you just had great sex	you were on a juice cleanse	you actually got sleep	you've made millions as a hand model
Essential equation	big hair + healthy flush + bee-stung lips	vitamin C serum + moisturizing cleanser + hair shine	white eye pencil + concealer + shimmer	exfoliator + overnight gloves + shellac mani
My fave picks to try (all available at amazon.com)	Oribe Dry Texturizing Spray gets out the greasies and gives sexy, I-earned-this-bedhead volume. Use a cream blush like Nars Penny Lane on the apples of your cheeks, and use DuWop Lip Venom for kissed-all-night lips. Someone definitely got laid.	Apply Kiehl's Powerful-Strength Line-Reducing Concentrate overnight with Aveeno Positively Radiant Brightening Cleanser in the A.M. Shine up that mane with Kérastase Elixir Ultime Versatile Beautifying Oil. Wow. You look good enough to blend into a kale smoothie.	Use Tarte EmphasEYES Inner Rim Brightener in Nude for an eye-opening wake-up call. Pat on undereye concealer like Shiseido Perfecting Stick, and finish with a dot of Bobbi Brown Shimmer Wash Eye Shadow in Bone in the inner corners of your eyes.	Apply an exfoliator like L'Occitane shea oil One Minute Hand Scrub with a fab bathing mitt like Baiden Mitten. For twenty minutes or more, slip on Bliss Glamour Gloves. Finish with a shellac polish in a peachy-pinky hue like CND Powder My Nose to elongate your digits. Handy!

Carson Confession: THE BARBIE PROJECT

I'll never forget when Oprah flew me out to Edmonton, the capital city of Alberta, Canada during the dead of winter (Thanks, O!), to do a "makeunder" for her show. I was given no information about Dawn, except her address. When Dawn opened the door, my face froze . . . and not because it was minus forty degrees outside. Standing before me was Malibu Barbie. With a radioactive orange tan, balloon sculpture lips, blinding-white teeth, masses of bleached-blond extensions, and 800-cc breast implants that would make a Hooters waitress look positively puny, all she needed to complete her look was Skipper and a bright pink convertible.

As Dawn led me into her home, I asked myself: How did this woman go from fantastic to plastic? What pushed her over the edge? And how were we going to get her back? Dawn was a forty-something suburban housewife with two teenage kids. Her looks had gotten her a lot of attention, and she liked it. Even kids on the school bus told her children their mom was a MILF. (Did I mention I had to school O on the definition of MILF?) To Dawn, this acronym was kind of a compliment. She almost seemed proud of the title. But when we went in the bathroom and started taking everything off, from her acrylic nails to her hair extensions, her faux-happy smile came off, too . . . and she had a complete meltdown.

It was then that Dawn told me her real story. She never felt pretty growing up and was teased in high school for being a flat-chested wallflower. As soon as she could, she beat it out of her small town, got a job, and started buying sexier clothes. All of a sudden, people were saying, "Wow, you look hot." Then she got a boob job and people said, "Wow, you look amazing," and that little positive reinforcement launched a destructive chain of bigger, bustier, bolder, blonder. So she found herself overdoing everything, from getting more breast augmentation to buying sluttier clothes to going from having a funky manicure to five-inch-long talons. Her highlighted hair had to keep getting whiter and longer, her lips more Jessica Rabbit-like.

When we aired the segment, O asked me, "Why do you think she did it?" I said it was her crutch, her addiction. Some people turn to drugs, some to alcohol. For Dawn, it was overdoing herself in hopes that people would like and accept her. It was then that Oprah and I had our own a-ha moment that you can have an addiction to self-improvement, and when insecurity is driving those improvements, it's hard to stop the cycle. Dawn was an extreme example of a woman dressing not for herself but as a shield, which is anything but empowering. But as sure as peanut butter will get gum out of your hair (does it?), we had a solution!

Our goal wasn't to change Dawn into a soccer mom—she still had that seductive vibe that worked for her in the very beginning—but we wanted her to reclaim the naturalness she'd lost.

Once we stripped everything away, it suddenly clicked. Her transformation was so jaw-dropping that when she walked onstage, everybody gasped.

With tears rolling down her face, Dawn uttered the words, "I feel like I'm presentable for my kids now." MILF now stood for "Mom Is Looking Fabulous."

MODERATION, *please!*

Like eating flourless chocolate cake and Googling "Channing Tatum Strip Tease," every good thing has its limits.

As you've just learned, kitten, it's easy to hop on the transformation train and miss your stop . . . and wind up in a place where you don't recognize your old self. I shared the Barbie story with you not to skeeve you out, but to show that the key to updating your look is to keep it real. Oftentimes, people need a little bit of a makeover and a bit of a makeunder. Let's say your hair is fried from years of single processes and needs a break from peroxide, so warmer highlights could be your answer to looking less harsh. But maybe your skin needs a youthful boost, and a little bit of filler and a quality bronzer is a winning combo that wakes up your whole face. Or your smile may really benefit from getting veneers, but you've been wearing the same dark lipstick and thick eyeliner for years and need a professional makeup-counter visit to lighten up your palette.

While you've learned there are a handful of improvements at your disposal, makeovers—like 18-karat-gold gangsta grillz—are not one-size-fits-all. I know it can be overwhelming to know which upgrades to pick and choose, so take it slow. Maybe your game plan will be trying a spray tan and buying a pair of Spanx. Or highlights and a little lash tinting. That's great! Think about what's bothering you most or what's most intriguing to you, start from there, and be willing to tweak as needed. Don't feel pressured to tackle every single change immediately, as if your Apple watch were set with a makeover-by-midnight alarm. Remember, it's only self-improvement if it improves your quality of life. Deep thoughts with Carson!

Now before you turn the page, can you give me just a minute to mix myself up an Emergen-C mocktail, because I'll need the extra energy to help you tackle a key part of your transformation: taming your closet. See you in a jiffy!

- -

BUTT *seriously . . .*
Sometimes the best statement is an understatement. If you're going to play up smoky eyes, pair them with a nude lip. If you're sporting serious cleavage, wear cigarette pants instead of a mini. It's all about yin and yang.

- -

Underdone	Well Done	Over the Top
mousy hair	subtle, face-framing color	double process in platinum . . . plus extensions
corncob teeth	whitened teeth	Chiclet teeth
upper-lip fur	waxing your upper lip	lasering your entire body
animal hair on your clothes	animal-print bra or clutch	animal-print bodysuit
pasty, pale skin	self-tanner or bronzer one shade darker than your natural shade	deepest setting on tanning booth or a Snooki spray tan
short, bitten nails	gel manicure	acrylics that look like Frito corn chips

"The promised land!"

2.

Out with the OLD . . .
In with the OOH!

*I like my money right where I can see it . . .
hanging in my closet.*

CARRIE BRADSHAW, *SEX AND THE CITY*

MY VERY FIRST BRUSH WITH A celebrity closet wowed me to the point where I practically needed to be resuscitated. I had run into Ellen DeGeneres at a party and we exchanged pleasantries and compliments on each other's blazers, and she invited me over to her house the next day. She gave me the grand tour and, of course, it ended with two gay blond television personalities back in the closet. This was over a decade ago, when giant closets weren't the norm, so the fact that the closet was the size of a regular bedroom made it seem positively palatial. I felt like Columbus discovering America, the haute and holy land. It wasn't just Ellen's wardrobe that had me transfixed—it was the way everything was displayed and stored. It looked like a Prada boutique, with a center island and fabulous lighting. Clean-lined jackets and pants were hung by hue and illuminated inside pristine glass cabinets. I couldn't touch them, but I whispered lovingly to her suit separates through the glass like a family member speaking to a loved one in prison.

My second celebrity-closet encounter happened while I was doing a Caress body-wash campaign with Kim Kardashian. We were in a bathtub together (nothing happened, Kanye!) but the most erotic part for me, of course, was peering into Kim's closet, or should I say, heavenly walk-in wardrobe. I floated among racks and racks of Herve Leger bandage dresses, oodles of nude Loubis with their trademark red soles, and a handbag homage to Louis Vuitton, Hermès, Chanel, and Chloe, all with matching dust bags. What I found interesting was that the emphasis was less on clothes than it was on well-organized accessories. Bags, shoes, belts, and jewelry were positioned in the forefront, easily visible to the eye. They were the centerpieces of her outfits, not the supporting cast. It was clear that one of Kim's secret weapons is letting great accessories truly inspire the look. The clever way her closet was arranged made it all so easy.

That's really what this chapter is all about: clearing the outdated and unworkable elements from your closet and transforming it into a glamorous, thoughtfully edited space, ready to fill with fun, interchangeable pieces that make you up-to-the-minute chic. Now here's the homeworky part. To do that, you've gotta give some things the

boot—maybe even your boots. I know you've depended on those black leather rock stars to get you everywhere, but if they're starting to look like deflated tires, it's time. Add to that the dress from last decade that you're holding on to "just in case," rows of blah tops that you skip over each morning, and cardigans that would look better repurposed as mini Doberman sweaters. Time to let those pieces go the way of the landlines and Diet Crystal Pepsi. Tossing those pieces you've clung to for years can be unnerving but also totally liberating. Here's how to whip your wardrobe into shape, starting with my favorite closet-cleaning solutions.

Kim's well-outfitted closet was an accessory junkie's Xanadu.

glamsform YOUR CLOSET

Use your clean-out project as a good excuse to simultaneously upgrade your closet. If it's dark and drab, how can you expect to enjoy getting dressed each morning?

ADD DRAMA	Which color makes you feel happy and glamorous? Try a high-gloss paint in silver, jade, peacock blue, tangerine, or plum.	Line shelves and drawers with tailored liners from containerstore.com. Pick natural fibers, plush fabric, or even scented ones.	Choose a graphic wallpaper, DIY-framed shopping bags from high-end boutiques, or vintage pics of chic gals striking poses (think Slim Aarons photo prints on onekingslane.com)
LIGHT IT RIGHT	Add a sleek flush-mount fixture or chandelier. Keep it at 40 watts to add ambience. Bonus points for a disco ball!	Pick up LED light strips from ikea.com to install in drawers, cabinets, and boot storage areas. It's not sexy light, but you need to see what you own, right?	Make like a Broadway starlet and install a panel of soft lightbulbs around your mirror for a flattering, diffused glow.
MAKE IT USER-FRIENDLY	Add a sleek and feminine chair, stool, or bench so you're creating a new lounge area.	Put a permanent spot for an iPhone docking station. A little "Uptown Funk" can only help an outfit come together.	Showcase your favorite shoes and handbags (stuff them with dust bags or tissue to keep their shape) at eye level.

Tszuj Do It...

Turn a room you don't really use (your grown child's bedroom or extra guest bedroom) into a five-star closet with a dramatic fainting sofa. Pretty! Who cares if it's down the hall; it will become your favorite escape. Add a minibar! Fill it with champers!

BUTT seriously...

Invest in the Container Store Long Underbed Box with Wheels. One comfortably fits two areas for sweaters plus bedding you won't use during the spring and summer. For delicate items, try an Archival Underbed Garment Storage Box, which comes with acid-free tissue (containerstore.com).

THE Ten-Step CLOSET ENEMA

A toxic closet is like a toxic friendship. You walk into it feeling hopeful, but the more time you spend in it, the worse you feel about yourself. Time to do one big flush. Hey, at least I'm not suggesting a *coffee* enema. . . .

WHAT YOU'LL NEED

A full face of makeup and hair (otherwise your try-ons will bomb)

Two rolling racks from Bed Bath & Beyond ($59.99 each)

Two extra-large garbage bags labeled "Hell No" and "Maybe"

Cardboard box

Frappuccino

Plastic "Loony Bin"

Swiffer

1. RACK IT UP

Take a gulp of Frappuccino. Ready? Move batches of clothing by group (pants first, then tops, blazers, sweaters, dresses, and so on) to your rolling racks so you can get a clear view. Chances are you'll be shocked by at least two things you find (I once discovered an ancient artifact in mine: balled-up acid-washed Cavariccis). Since I love anything with a dual purpose, your racks can double as air-dry-only stations for delicate laundry in the future. Or Olympic uneven bars for your niece's American Girl dolls. Told you I was practical!

2. SIMPLIFY

Reshop your rolling rack items as if you were browsing the racks at a store. Would you try this on today? If your upper lip starts to curl, toss it in the "Hell No" pile. If you're debating, try it on with good undergarments, shoes, the works. Does it work? Are you making excuses for it like, "Well, I spent so much on this . . . I should keep it." Honey, so-so equals no.

3. MOVE YOUR "MAYBES"

You may truly be on the fence with some seasonal items, like that wool blazer you can't decide on because it's summer and eighty-five degrees outside. Relocate a select group of seasonal "maybes" to another closet in your home and go back to it with fresh eyes three months later. If you try it on then and don't feel great in it, it's an automatic no. Note: If you're still having a tough time shedding your "maybes," see my swap-meet party tip.

- - - - - - - - - - - - - - - - - - - -

Tszuj Do It . . . Hold a swap meet of style at different girlfriends' houses. The price of admission: a great appetizer. Pour margaritas, browse, carouse, and do closet fashion shows for each other, á la *Sex and the City*. Swap outfits you're so over, but no seller's remorse!

- - - - - - - - - - - - - - - - - - - -

4. CLEAR THE FLOOR

Half of the reason closets look so cluttered is because there's too much lurking on the ground, from shoes to bags to . . . Wait—is that a Thighmaster back there? Take another energizing sip of Frappuccino, clear the clutter, and Swiff yourself into an OCD frenzy. Put shoes in vertical storage compartments (or at least a low rack that elevates them off the floor) and move all dust-gathering items to upper shelving.

5. EMPLOY THE TWO-YEAR BOOT

Haven't worn it in the last two years? Out it goes

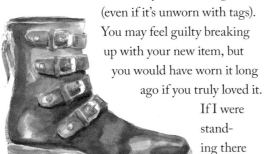

(even if it's unworn with tags). You may feel guilty breaking up with your new item, but you would have worn it long ago if you truly loved it. If I were standing there with you and your clothes, I'd look at them and say, "She's just not that into you."

"Seriously, you're kicking me out? We've been sole mates since Lilith Fair."

6. LOSE DIET-CONTINGENT DUDS

If you have to qualify any piece of clothing with, "I just need to lose ten pounds to fit into this," or "Well, if I just let this out an inch or two, it could work," it's a goner. Why have a constant reminder that you need to whittle yourself down? By the way, I advise going to the fridge right now and replenishing the whipped cream on your half-finished Frap. Live a little!

7. YOUTH-HOSTEL WEAR MUST GO

Baggy, holey, stretchy, faded, stained? Sayonara. Sometimes we wear things out, and that's okay. Ignore that little voice telling you that your tailor down the street can work miracles, or that "No one will notice that little snag/spot/hole!" It's o-v-a-h. Bye, Felicia! Don't forget to rethink your old pajamas, ratty sweats, and stretched-out workout clothing, too.

8. START SOLE SEARCHING

Try on all your shoes and belts with your more streamlined wardrobe. Whatever looks unflattering or is uncomfortable (did someone say "bunionectomy"?) goes into the cardboard box for giveaway. It's better to have fewer pairs of shoes but ones you love that fit properly. Like my Playboy-mansion–ready velvet loafers. Still waiting on that invite, Hef!

9. TRY SUITCASE LIVING

Take out your ten favorite items and five favorite accessories and only live with those pieces for a week. You'll see how little you actually need to get by and feel good. Then go back through your racks and weed out 10 percent more. You should only be left with items you absolutely love that are either on-trend or totally timeless.

10. MAKE ROOM FOR THE CRAZY

For items you can't part with but wear only on special/funky/random occasions (like my tropical fruit tuxedo or Catholic-schoolgirl Halloween costume), relocate them to their own bizarre zone (aka your plastic "Loony Bin" on a high shelf or a garment bag in another closet) so you don't have to sift through that visual noise on a daily basis.

carson confession: GIRL, THAT'S GOTTA GO!

destination: donation bin!

It's always amazing to me how hard it is to let go of clothing we actually hate. I remember doing a closet covert attack (truly, that's the only thing you could call this) with a woman named Shantelle in Atlanta. We were given advance notice that she was a bit of a hoarder, to the point where her closet looked on the brink of exploding. She had basically archived everything since her twenty-first birthday two decades earlier. When we started sifting through hanger after hanger, she got defensive, which turned into bitchy, à la, "Carson, what's wrong with THAT shirt? Yours isn't that great, either!"

No matter how hard we prodded, Shantelle wouldn't let go of anything, like a child with her stuffed animals. So we hit her with a tranquilizer dart and a shot of Benadryl. Just kidding—making sure you're still reading. We decided to take another approach. We called Shantelle's

two best friends over for a closet intervention. Since her friends were roughly the same size as her, we had *them* model her clothing. How's that for a perspective tweak? What started out as, "What? She looks great. I'm keeping it!" became, "Wow, you both look pretty bad!" Soon the ladies were cracking up and taking ussies in Shantelle's worst ensembles.

Sometimes all we need to do is get out of our own way and realize that more is not always more! Slowly, with Shantelle's blessing, we started making reject piles of tops, pants, skirts, shoes, purses . . . then she couldn't stop! Shantelle's watershed moment was when she said hasta la vista to her everyday bag (which looked like a patent-leather station wagon that could fit a pet armadillo) and later replaced it with a clean-lined tote from Coach that went with absolutely everything.

QUIZ: ARE YOU DRESSED FOR THIS DECADE?

1. Take me into your closet. Now pick up three favorite items. They make you feel:

   a. Hip.

   b. Comfortable.

   c. Sentimental.

2. Which of the following can be found in your jewelry box?

   a. Gold cuff.

   b. Charm bracelet.

   c. Pearl choker.

3. The latest fashion trends I see make me . . .

   a. Giddy. I'll follow ones that seem easy enough to replicate.

   b. Curious. I'll wait until I see friends wearing them first.

   c. Confused. Are these people smoking something?

4. The neckline of your favorite sweater is . . .

   a. Waterfall cardigan. A little sexy, a little snuggly.

   b. V-neck. Tried and true, it looks good on everyone.

   c. Mock turtleneck. Rock the mock.

5. When was your best era, when you looked and felt amazing?

   a. Every era is my best era!

   b. Somewhere between first getting married and today.

   c. High school.

BUTT *seriously* . . .
Remove all the plastic from your dry-cleaning pronto. Clothes like to breathe, too!

MOSTLY A'S: *Au Courant Chick*

You're not afraid to update and you welcome change, which is good for your style and your mental health. Just when you feel like you're settled into what works, you ask yourself if there's any way to spice it up. As long as you're not a trend slave, keep up the envelope pushing.

MOSTLY B'S: *Getting There, Gal*

You see what's out there but stick to the tried and true. It's okay to love your stand-the-test-of-time pieces, but don't be too safe. Shake it up with new shoes or bold jewelry. Your wardrobe shouldn't be your uniform . . . unless you're a hot forest ranger.

MOSTLY C'S: *Out-of-Date Diva*

Honey, the mock turtleneck species has long been extinct. Make your way into the millennium by taking a hard line with your wardrobe. What can be phased out? If you're swimming in a mountain of shoulder pads, it's time to simplify.

Tszuj Do It . . . Arrange your closet backward, with the "party up front and business in the back." Looking at sequins daily is proven to extend your life span by five years!

---

recycle YOUR WARDROBE ONLINE

Okay, you know some things must vacate the premises. Why not release those duds into the universe . . . and get something back? Not only will these sites help you be more eco-chic, you can cash in on those castoffs for brand-new ones. *Cha-ching!*

materialwrld.com

"Some boys kiss me / Some boys hug me / I think they're oka-a-ay / If they don't give me proper credit / I just walk away-yay." The materialwrld.com app totally understands that. They believe personal style is an evolution and we should keep the clothing life cycle going, which will reduce environmental impact . . . and score you a gift card! Here's how it works: Upload pics of your used clothing, wait for them to make an offer, mail in those pieces, and get compensated pronto (since this isn't consignment). They'll resell the clothes and make charitable donations, and in return, you'll get a gift card to a major department store, from Barneys to Saks to Bloomie's.

therealreal.com

I've recently become addicted to luxury online consignment jackpot therealreal.com. Own any designer items (think handbags, shoes, purses, clothing, jewelry) that are gathering dust in your closet but you just can't imagine tossing them? Ship out your duds for approval (check their list of accepted brands on their site first) or meet with a local rep who will advise you on what sells best on the site and ship it for you. You'll get a check for up to 70 percent of the price your item sells for, plus promotional gift cards to major department stores when you consign over ten items. You'll also get an additional 10 percent value if you choose to get paid with a gift card to one of their retail partners, like Neiman Marcus (the name I plan to give my first child, puppy, or Shopkin . . . whichever comes first).

thredup.com

When it comes to trading in your well-maintained, everyday clothes, thredUP.com is where it's at. Your items don't have to be prescreened, but you roll the dice as to whether they'll be accepted. Still, the odds are in your favor, since they acquire so many brand-name pieces you probably own (think J.Crew, Abercrombie, Gap, Kate Spade, Banana Republic). Order a Clean Out Kit from their Web site, fill up the bag they send you, and ship it out for free. They have a handy pricing calculator that helps you guesstimate what you'll potentially earn back. Two to four weeks later, you've either made money, or points toward a new purchase, or can give the proceeds as a charitable donation to one of thredUP's favorite causes, which as we all know, gives you amazing fashion karma.

- -

BUTT *seriously* . . .

Before consigning, dry-clean items, have minimal repairs done if necessary, and include all tags, dust bags, and original boxes if you still have them.

- -

BECOME A CONSIGNING Pro

If you don't have a local consignment shop that can sell your discarded duds, or if you want a wider reach than your hometown, try consigning online. I asked my lovely friends at therealreal.com for tips I could share with you, and here's what they had to say.

LOOK FOR CRITICAL MASS

More eyeballs yield a faster sell-thru in the world of e-commerce. So, before you choose a consignment partner, research the site traffic and reach of the Web site. Look for at least a two- to three-million-member base to drive a quick sale.

SELL TO THE RIGHT CUSTOMER

Look at the type of items being sold by the company you are considering consigning with. Do your items fit that equation? If not, seek out another venue. A luxury site won't take nondesigner items, so it pays to get insight into their customer demographic.

BEWARE OF HIDDEN FEES

What percent of the sale will you receive, minus the hidden fees? Some consignment stores give you 40 percent, some give you 50 percent, and online you can get 60–80 percent. If you attempt to sell your goods on your own or through an auction site, it may seem like you could earn more. However, hidden credit-card fees, processing costs, shipping, and returns will quickly diminish any profit.

AVOID RETURN HASSLES

Do you forfeit your commission if your pieces are returned? What if your items don't sell in six months' time? A site's return policy is critical to you as a consignor.

READ THE FINE PRINT FOR PAYMENT

Some online sites will give you points rather than cash, while others deduct additional fees, like credit-card processing fees. Some, like therealreal.com, offer a value option of an extra 10 percent when you choose gift-card payment over cash to one of their luxury retail partners. Understand when you will be paid and how you will be paid.

- -

BUTT seriously . . .

Take photos of all of your items before you consign. Insure your items so you have a record of what you sent should anything get lost in transit.

- -

- -

Tszuj Do It . . .

Order a fabric mannequin on amazon.com (yes, I really did just say that) and give it a diva name (that too). Dress it with items you're unsure about discarding or consigning, so you can see it from a "department store" perspective.

- - - - - - - - - - - - - - -

Hello! ♡ my name is Céline

Donation 101

Not giving back is whack! Sure, it's easier to just take a trip to the trash bin, but there's no excuse for tossing your "Hell No" bags. If you'd rather donate your clothing than recycle or consign it, here are some easy options that will give you the warm fuzzies . . . and a tax write-off:

donationtown.org

This nationwide charity donation pick-up program allows you to donate to hundreds of charities depending on your zip code, from Habitat for Humanity to Hospice to Big Brothers Big Sisters. Your donation is tax deductible, so don't forget to fill out that form.

dressforsuccess.org

One of my faves, this awesome organization gets women back on their feet in the workplace looking and feeling great, so park your gently used suits and professional-looking clothing from your "Hell No" bag here. Log on to the site to chat with a local affiliate about hosting a clothing drive in your area.

goodwill.org

Go "Goodwill Hunting" in your closet for items you're willing to part with, and become part of Goodwill's Donate Movement on donate.goodwill.org. Plug in the amount of items you donated and see how many hours of job-search class you made possible. You can also organize a donation drive for your community through this site.

pickupplease.org

Log on to this site to donate to the Vietnam Veterans of America. They'll come in twenty-four hours and pick up just about anything and everything you leave outside for them . . . except your shih tzu. Tax write-off perks included.

- -

BUTT *seriously* . . .

Download the "letgo" app (us.letgo.com) to your smartphone, which is gaining buzz as the new flea market for castoffs. Just stay on track as you're posting your clothing, or you'll wind up purchasing a used trampoline, a bearskin rug, and a Yamaha guitar before you've finished.

- -

MY love affair WITH LAUNDRY

Believe it or not, doing laundry is one of the great Zen joys of my life. Working in entertainment, a lot of times I'll tape something or work on a project and it's months before I see it come to life. With laundry, there's instant gratification: You do it, you fold it, you put it away. Here are my favorite essentials:

THE LAUNDRESS WOOL & CASHMERE SHAMPOO

You know how hair stylists tell you not to over-wash your hair so it doesn't strip out the natural oils that keep it lustrous and shiny? Cashmere is kind of the same way. The few times I've sent a cashmere or cashmere-blend sweater to the dry cleaner, the chemicals took the life out of it. I've brought it back to springy life by hand-washing in cold with The Laundress Wool & Cashmere Shampoo. If you're a dry-cleaning junkie like I used to be, get their Dry Cleaning Detox Kit, because we all need to detox one way or another (thelaundress.com).

SARD WONDER SOAP WITH EUCALYPTUS

I first fell for Australian stain sticks when a friend gifted me Exit Stain Stick, but it's impossible to find in the States, so I thankfully discovered its close cousin, Sard Wonder Soap with Eucalyptus (amazon.com). Along with koalas and Kylie Minogue, Sard is an Aussie gem. I work some in with a toothbrush as soon as I spot a stain, and I like that I can put it on up to a week before I wash. It gets out red wine, grease, boot polish, and blood—all the components of a crime scene . . . or a good party!

FAULTLESS SIZING

A lot of women don't realize the need for ironing because so many shirts are wrinkle-free poly blends. But when you're dealing with cotton (even your sheets) it's worth doing. Plain starch can make shirts too stiff, which is why I prefer Faultless Sizing Fabric Finish, an ironing additive that comes in a spray can (faultless.com). It has a retro design that makes me feel like I'm a 1940s movie heroine ironing the shirts of her drunken husband who could come home at any moment!

ROWENTA STEAMER

I am a huge advocate of owning a great steamer—Botox for your clothes, with no downtime. I have an outlet in my closet and plug in my commercial Rowenta Precision Valet Garment Steamer with a built-in hanger anytime my shirts need a morning or evening pick-me-up. For travel, a portable steamer is an easy alternative to overspending on hotel laundry services (save your cash for pillaging the minibar). I love my Rowenta DR6015 Ultrasteam Brush that comes with a travel pouch. Just remember to dump out every drop of water before you pack it. Both steamers are available at bedbathandbeyond.com. (You know you have a 20-percent-off coupon lurking somewhere that you've been dying to use.)

CLUELESS
No More!

Now that you've broken up with all the items that weren't working in your wardrobe, it's time to prep your closet for new additions. You can't go wrong by following in the footsteps of Cher from *Clueless*, my favorite nineties Oscar winner (*as if!*). Now it's time for the postmillennial version.

TURN YOUR CLOSET INTO A BOUTIQUE

With all of Cher's looks computerized for mix-and-matchability through her amazing closet system, building a well-edited wardrobe was a snap. Categorize your remaining threads by clothing type and color: Think groups of blazers, print tops, jeans, dresses. Space out items with two to three inches between hangers so you can actually see what you own . . . and what you need.

LOG YOUR LOOKS

Imagine having your entire wardrobe organized on your phone (sanity!). Yes, it takes forever, since you need to import pics individually, but stay with it, because Stylebook (stylebookapp.com) is totally worth the time and $3.99. The app acts as your virtual closet, helping you pull together daily looks by dragging clothing, shoes, and

other accessories to create complete outfits (with a white edited background so your items look *InStyle*-worthy), as well as brainstorming new outfits via online retailers.

Plus, you can track how frequently you've worn certain pieces, plan outfits ahead using Stylebook's handy calendar tool with mini clothing icons, learn which items you never wear (back to the donation bin!), and find out not only which articles of clothing have the best cost-per-usage factor but the total value of your closet. Surprise, surprise: I learned that mine's worth more than my apartment. Oops.

- -

BUTT *seriously* . . .
Back everything up on the iCloud so your closet actually transfers when you upgrade to a new phone—or drop yours in the toilet.

- -

EDIT LIKE A FASHION EDITOR

If you find yourself scrambling to put an outfit together on weekday mornings and don't feel like scrolling through your phone for pics, photograph outfit combos in advance, old-school style. I have the most adorbs white Fujifilm Instax Mini (they're everywhere from Walmart to Urban Outfitters) that pops out smaller vertical pics, which are perfect for tucking around a full-length mirror.

long sleeve

2"-3" SPACE!

Blazers

maxis

print tops

jeans

boots

shoes

Closet Boutique

Create a total look by snapping your favorite tailored pants and skirts with tops and blazers, and don't forget the bag, the bangle, and the shoes. Be ruthless! Only shoot things you know work, like skinny jeans and a black blazer with a crisp white shirt and gold bangles. Think of it as making advance "pulls" for your own magazine shoot, like the editors do.

MAKE MOMMIE DEAREST PROUD

Swap out your wire hangers, because you know how cranky they made Joan Crawford. Try Mawa EuroCurve hangers from amazon.com. They have a gentle curve that won't give your treasured tops, sweaters, and blazers bat-wing shoulders. Make space for new purchases with a fifty-pack of Neat-freak Felt Clothes Hangers from walmart.com.

Tszuj Do It . . . When I bought my apartment, my real estate agent got me monogrammed hangers as a housewarming gift. Presto change-o, my closet turned into a Brooks Brothers store awaiting square-jawed, floppy-haired models toting croquet mallets! Create your own design at hangerstore.com.

BUTT *seriously . . .*
I always keep a haberdashery brush in my laundry kit. It's an old-school tool that I use for brushing hats, suede jackets, wool blazers, pony-hair purses, boots, and other nonwashable, textured fabrics that need freshening but not a full dry-cleaning treatment. I recommend the Kent Handcrafted Clothes Brush (amazon.com).

GETTING *Inspired*

Your closet is streamlined and glammed up, and your remaining pieces are well taken care of. Now you're ready to just add fabulousness. How do you know what you even like, or where to begin? Start fueling your brain with fresh style intel.

LET IT RIP

My Ralph Lauren styling days were often filled with the sound of magazine pages ripping. All of us stylists would devour mag after mag, from *Vogue* (high concept) to *InStyle* (totally practical) to *Garden & Gun* (super styling). The goal was an array of images that we could tear out and put in our three-ring style binders. It's old-school, but try it! Even interior design magazines can tip you off to colors and patterns you might not have thought about incorporating into your wardrobe.

PIN LIKE A MADWOMAN

What I love most about Pinterest and Instagram is that no matter where you live or what you do, you can give and get inspiration. Maybe you'll wind up following a stylist from Madrid who opens your eyes to designs you never had access to. It's just a matter of diving in. Instead of clothing, which can be daunting from the sheer amount of options, start with the images that most inspire you. Maybe it's Paris, or paint colors, or even beautifully plated food. Start there and let it lead you to pull in clothing that completes the story. Since it's more addictive than Splenda, you'll wind up building and building. You could be the next inter-Web sensation!

MAKE A STYLE LIBRARY

Now it's time to divvy your online inspiration pics into style files and be more deliberate. Maybe one file is dedicated to winter, with your prime picks for vests, boots, bags, and coats (with your dream log cabin, a video clip about cold-weather fashion, and a hot toddy recipe thrown in for fun). Another page could be devoted to work wear, another for the color greige, and so on. Soon you'll have a library of looks stored in your phone *and* your subconscious, which makes it easier to spot items you actually know you want when you're shopping offline. Plus, you can get alerts when items you pin go on sale.

GET THE STYLE DOWNLOAD

Mandating what to read in the blogosphere is tricky: Personal style blogs are more personal than the shows you choose to binge-watch (aren't they?), and one person's dream stream of daily outfits could be another's Web nightmare. So I'll leave that up to you. But these sites are good places to get inspired by fashion in general.

fashionista.com

In their shopping section you'll get tons of intel on how to shop the best online sales, plus the number of shares each link has already racked up.

whowhatwear.com

My favorite part of this site is the Street Style section, where real-girl pics merge with practical tips that anyone can adopt—like what to wear with your turquoise jewelry, or twenty ways to wear a scarf.

net-a-porter.com

Aspirational inspiration! The clothes, the accessories, even the tech items are so yummy, a hit of glamorama viewing is all I need. Let the trends you see on this site, from a Tabitha Simmons wedge sandal to a spiked Christian Dior iPad case, guide you when you shop Macy's or Dillard's or Lord & Taylor. PS: Their magazines, *Porter* and *The Edit*, are fab reads.

polyvore.com

I come here to see what's trending. Like Pinterest, Tumblr, and others, you can get a taste of how multiple looks come together and comment on them if you're feeling sassy. You can also find "sets" created by users based on a search term like "navy-and-white-striped shirt." That means tons of fresh ideas on how to shop your closet and what to do with random accessories you already own.

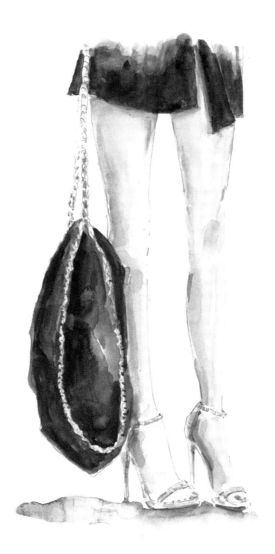

CHOOSE YOUR Muse

There's a reason why fashion designers often credit their muses with the success of their collections, from Sofia Coppola for Marc Jacobs to Julianne Moore for Tom Ford. Or my personal favorite, Nacho Figueras for Ralph Lauren—I'll ride that pony any day. With a package, er, face and a persona to be inspired by, it's so much easier to pull together a series of cohesive looks that stay on point. So ask yourself, *Who is* my *muse?* Everyone has a style icon they admire, whom you feel weirdly connected to and influenced by whenever you catch sight of him or her. The person doesn't have to be famous, the same sex as you, or even among the living! (They should be human, though.)

Now look around your closet and ask yourself how much of it reflects how you'd like to be perceived. Let's say you've accrued way too many Juicy sweatsuits over the years and want to look more polished and less *Mob Wives.* Or you got sucked into the preppy vortex and want to ease out of those cable knits and into some mohair. Ask yourself, *WW-MMD? (What would my muse do?)*

The best part about an imaginary muse is you can take her or him on all of your retail excursions. You think I'm kidding, but Grace Kelly is my secret shopping partner in crime. If I could imagine her scrunching her nose at any of my picks, I give those items a second thought. It's not about copying your muse to a T or breaking the bank to buy the same brands the muse wears, but taking elements of his or her style to help you focus on how you want to project yourself to the world. Just don't tell your muse about it . . . unless it's me. Stalker!

Tszuj Do It . . . Next time you hit the mall, take on your muse's persona. Choose your items as if you were them. What would she select? What would he veto? And most importantly, what would your muse order from Panda Express?

So, ladies, let's recap: You have a pared-down, ultraorganized wardrobe ready to expand. But you know that it requires more than a binge buying session to truly land on the essence of your new style, which is why you're going to do your Pinterest homework and start inspiration hunting. You're going to channel your ultimate muse. It's not so much about leading you to specific items, but moving toward an evolution of your personal look. You don't want to make a full-on fashion update overnight, so just have fun pushing ahead with purpose. One week it could be conquering your ultimate dark denim jeans, and the next month it might be cultivating your neutral hobo or statement necklace. Just add as you go, whenever the mood strikes you. That's the whole idea of shoes and jewelry and clothing. It's girly and it's fun and it should make you feel good—not pressured to do a complete 180. Are we ready to start slowly building? I'll take that nod and second Chardonnay pour as a yes.

BUTT *seriously . . .*
Remember that great *Domino* magazine column called, "Turn My Outfit into a Room"? Find your favorite Pinterest pic and do the reverse.

carson confession: PAGING GRACE KELLY

In case you were wondering, my lifelong muse is Grace Kelly. We are both natural (!) blond Scorpios born in Pennsylvania one day apart, forty years apart, which means absolutely nothing and absolutely everything. Her poise, her regal mane, her sharply tailored style, her ability to rock any accessory as if it had been made for her is my definition of perfection. I find myself thinking WWMMD when I put together an outfit. Maybe I'll answer that by subtracting a belt that is "too much," or adding a pocket scarf that feels tszuj right. And just for giggles and goose bumps, I'll tell you a short story: I once starred in a stage production of *The Drowsy Chaperone* and was so jittery before getting onstage that I popped into an antiques store for retail therapy. Lo and behold, the owner of the store approached me and said, "I have something for you." He unlocked a drawer and removed a book and handed it to me. I opened it up, and inside was an inscription from none other than the princess of Monaco. Holy Hermès! My muse was coaching me from the other side.

3.

I Just LOVE
a Woman in Uniform

BRAVO. YOU'VE SUCCESSFULLY PURGED your tired, outworn, and underutilized clothing and have found them a happy new home. Now that you've kissed those items bye-bye, it's time to buy-buy! The trick is to ensure everything's going to work together, like a finely tuned style uniform, so you're always going to look like your clothes are going to the same party. It makes getting dressed in the morning so much easier because you can put on your bottom, your top, and a topper like your blazer or cashmere cardigan, then throw on different accessories for that day and you're done.

I know thinking of your clothes as a uniform sounds super boring, but many of the chicest people in the world have a style uniform—you just may not have noticed. Michael Kors is always in a tummy-slimming dark T and blazer with dark or white jeans, a great statement watch, and aviators. Anna Wintour relies on A-line skirts and structured tops that show off her toned arms, and finishes her look with fitted coats, nude heels, and bold sunglasses. Even Oprah has a uniform of color and texture that always involves a strong,

face-framing neckline that highlights her smile, and a cinched-in waist to give her a fabulous shape.

Uniform dressing is the most practical way of getting dressed, but it can still have fun, unpredictable elements to shake things up. I like to think of it as the best kind of dinner party: You have regulars who always make you feel comfortable, with a few spicy additions and wild cards thrown in for color. Even with the same uniform, every woman is going to rock it differently with her own personal spin. When you eventually find out what your ideal combos are, you can kick them up or dress them down, depending on where the day or night takes you. And I hope the night takes you somewhere great . . . and I get to be your plus one!

Here are some basics to get you started—I call them Twenty-five Easy Pieces. Don't feel like you have to purchase everything new, because you probably have half of these pieces in your closet already.

When I started in fashion, I had already adopted the sailor-striped sweater as my uniform; that way, I wouldn't have to drive myself crazy trying to figure out what to wear.

JEAN PAUL GAULTIER

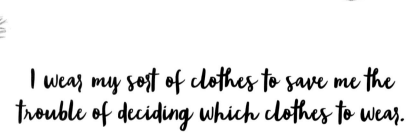

I wear my sort of clothes to save me the trouble of deciding which clothes to wear.

KATHARINE HEPBURN

twenty-five easy pieces:
BUILD YOUR STYLE UNI!

Think of these items as your chocolate or vanilla FroYo, and the fun toppings (i.e., accessories) come later for tszuj-ing.

PANTS

Dark denim

White jeans

Skinny black pants

Black leggings

TOPS

Tunic

Crisp white shirt

Black rayon blend top

Sleeveless layering tank

Printed long-sleeve blouse

SWEATERS

Neutral cashmere cardigan

Black turtleneck

Thin layering "summer-weight" sweater in neutral

DRESSES/SKIRTS

Maxi dress

Wrap dress

Little black dress

Navy or black stretch pencil skirt

OUTERWEAR

Fitted blazer in white and in black or navy

Leather jacket (think minimal and sleek)

Wool peacoat

SHOES

Ankle boots in brown

Black boots with heel

Gold strappy sandals

Nude heels

Wedges

Flats in neutral

forty CHIC COMBINATIONS

Look at all the different looks you can create with your Twenty-five Easy Pieces:

DAYTIME

Dark denim + white shirt + blazer + flats

Dark denim + rayon top + leather jacket + black boots

Dark denim + tunic + wedges

Dark denim + turtleneck + peacoat + black boots

Dark denim + printed blouse + blazer + brown boots

Leggings + tunic + flats

Leggings + layering sweater + leather jacket + flats

Maxi dress + cashmere cardi + wedges

Pencil skirt + white top + thin layering sweater + nude heels

Skinny black pants + tunic + wedges

White jeans + tunic + wedges

White jeans + printed blouse + nude heels

White jeans + white shirt + cashmere cardi + brown boots

White jeans + tank + leather jacket + flats

White jeans + layering sweater + brown boots

NIGHTTIME

Dark denim + rayon top + leather jacket + nude heels

Dark denim + printed blouse + blazer + strappy sandals

LBD + cashmere cardi + nude heels

LBD + leather jacket + strappy sandals

Pencil skirt + printed blouse + strappy sandals

Pencil skirt + tank + blazer + nude heels

Skinny black pants + rayon top + leather jacket + strappy sandals

Skinny black pants + tank + blazer + strappy sandals

Skinny black pants + printed blouse + nude heels

Skinny black pants + black rayon top + strappy sandals

White jeans + tank + blazer + strappy sandals

Wrap dress + cashmere cardi + nude heels

Wrap dress + leather jacket + strappy sandals

Dark denim + printed blouse + leather jacket + black boots

Dark denim + rayon blouse + peacoat + flats

Leggings + tank + cashmere cardi + black boots

Maxi dress + leather jacket + wedges

Pencil skirt + white shirt + nude heels

Pencil skirt + printed blouse + nude heels

Skinny black pants + white shirt + blazer + flats

Skinny black pants + black turtleneck + peacoat + flats

Skinny black pants + tank + blazer + flats

White jeans + black turtleneck + leather jacket + black boots

Wrap dress + flats

Wrap dress + black boots

Each woman needs to know herself and think that the clothes are here to make her more beautiful, because the person is more important than the clothes. . . . I do so many things— so most of the time it's like a uniform. Of course, I buy new stuff; I love fashion, but I have a look now— I don't change so much.

CARINE ROITFELD

YOUR Seven STYLE-UNIFORM STAPLES

When you're buying your Twenty-five Easy Pieces, the focus should be on fabric and quality but also on a flattering fit that shows off your best features, from strong legs to a great chest. Here are tips for the top seven players in your style uniform:

1. MAXI DRESS

When you find the perfect maxi, it'll be one of your most versatile pieces. Pair it with great jewelry for a daytime date, throw on flip-flops and a fedora for your vacation, and add a jean jacket, wedges, and hobo bag for casual workdays. Let's maximize your maxi purchase:

Seek Out Structure

You want a built-in waist detail like a panel, belt, or side-tie sash that creates a waistline—otherwise it can look like a maternity dress. Choose one with a built-in bra or wide enough straps to enable you to wear one. (In the design world we call this "bra-friendly.") If you're okay with wearing a strapless bra, a crisscross halter can draw eyes to your clavicle, which is an attractive feature on just about everyone. Skip halter styles with teardrop or triangle holes in the cleavage, though. They're a little hoochie-town, hon.

Keep the Pattern and Print Quiet

We're all pattern crazy now, and it's what retailers are pushing, but in a maxi, all that fabric can be too much like a psychedelic tie-dye or Pottery Barn tablecloth. Go for details in the cut, instead. Some have short sleeves that draw your eyes away from the arms and to a V-shaped bust. Wrap styles can give your dress movement, while ruching can be ultraslimming.

Mind Your Hemline

A hemline that falls higher in the center and gives a peek at your calves and fabulous shoes (because you're not wearing sneaks here) can be flattering. For standard styles, tailor the hemline to fall just at your anklebone. If it shows too much ankle, it'll cut you off like a capri pant can, but too long and you'll look lost in it.

Embrace Fake Fibers

Sometimes we get scared and think man-made fibers are not chic and not cool, but a Lycra-polyester-spandex combo just works. Great synthetics give you weight, and with maxis, it's all about the weight. If it's lightweight cotton, it can look cheap and be too see-through when the sun hits you. Too heavy and it can feel like a robe made of scuba-diving material. I love Michael Kors's Michael line for great options in polyester/elastane (especially for curvy ladies), and Diane von Furstenberg stretch-knit maxis. Both are available at major department stores like Macy's, Nordstrom, and Saks.

2. LITTLE BLACK DRESS

There's a reason why the LBD (or "little black dress"), originally dubbed "Chanel's Ford," has been in vogue since 1926. Everyone from Audrey Hepburn to Jennifer Aniston relies on this always-chic wardrobe staple to slim, define, and project simple elegance. The LBD is timeless, always on-trend, and ready for rock-star embellishments.

> Black is the most slimming of all colors. It is the most flattering. You can wear black at any time. You can wear it at any age. You can wear it for almost any occasion. I could write a book about black.
>
> **CHRISTIAN DIOR**

Try Asymmetric

An asymmetric hem can be flattering to fabulous legs, and it's not the only place it pays to be off-kilter. An asymmetric neckline is great for big busts because it drapes over the chest instead of clinging to it. For medium to smaller busts, open-chest styles with geometric cut-ins are flattering because they bring attention to the clavicle and slim out the arms. It also gives a more modern look overall, especially with a color-block pattern. Roland Mouret and Victoria Beckham are the king and queen of geo-cuts, but you can find affordable versions from DKNY, Tahari, and Halston Heritage (bloomingdales.com and neimanmarcus.com).

Disguise as Needed

The LBD can be a great disguiser. If you have heavier arms, go with an illusion sleeve or three-quarter sexy lace sleeve. Bigger bum? Hippy? Emphasize your small waist with an A-line silhouette. If you have narrow hips, stick to a straight sheath style that hits just at the knee and gives your tush some shape. Chiffon and silk slip styles may look pretty on a hanger, but think about the magic of internal structure: You can minimize your middle with a paneled design that has belly-smoothing effects.

Get Strap-Happy

Unless you're a willowy dancer, strapless and spaghetti-strap styles can make your upper half look doughy and just aren't as flattering as a neckline with more structure. Better choice: an elegant bateau neckline, a wide-paneled style that flutters out just beyond your shoulders, or a flattering V that looks good on everyone.

- -

Tszuj Do It . . . Have fun with embellishments in beading, lace, and real and faux leather. LBD should not stand for Little Bit Dull! And if you find a designer that makes the perfect LBD for you, why not try one in color? It may not be quite as slimming, but the fun factor of color more than makes up for that.

- -

3. CASHMERE CARDIGAN

Cardis are hard to wear because they're inherently nerdy, frumpy, and bulky. Are you thinking of *Ugly Betty*, too? Sweaters with strategic cuts and feather-light knits are going to be much more flattering. If you can't splurge on a 100 percent cashmiracle, a cashmere blend works, too.

Start with the Silhouette

The waterfall cardigan, which drapes down in the front, has a fluid, lengthening effect. Hands down, it's the most universally flattering silhouette and always looks modern. I love charcoal, heather gray, taupe, and camel as neutrals. Free People makes a good waterfall in multiple hues (lordandtaylor.com); Wyatt has a straight-edge, color-blocked version (bluefly.com); and Style & Co. (macys.com) offers a ruffle-trim version for a slightly more feminine look. (Superaffordable noncashmere versions are always available at qvc.com or hsn.com.)

Seek Out Slimming Arms

Knitwear stretched too tightly can make upper arms resemble kielbasa sausage. The most attractive styles are thin, lightweight knits that skim over your shape without clinging to bulges. Nix anything that has a cable knit running through the upper arm, as it'll add bulk.

Ban Bad Details

Buttons, toggles, and big pockets are best left to Kathy Bates in *Misery.* Besides, who else really needs room for a hammer? The simpler the design, the better.

- -

BUTT *seriously . . .*

Look for cardigans with a double-thick knit on the body of the sweater and a thinner knit on the arm—an instant upper-arm slimmer.

- -

4. CRISP WHITE SHIRT

Ever notice how hot guys look in just a great tailored white shirt and jeans? Well, it works for women, too. White is a winning color on everybody, especially near the face. It makes your teeth and your eyes look whiter and always looks fresh under a sweater or fitted blazer.

Say Yes to Stretch

Like maxi dresses, don't discount a touch of man-made in your blend. A shirt with a poly blend is going to give you coverage, conform better to your body, and hold a crisper shape than 100 percent cotton. My favorite is a stretch poplin with a blend of cotton, nylon, and elastane. High-end manufacturers like Prada, as well as designers like me, use this blend on their white shirts, so you know you're buying right.

Whatever you want it to be, the white shirt becomes. The most important thing is the fit. If it fits well, and you like the way it looks you can accessorize it with diamonds or with nothing. It's up to you.

CAROLINA HERRERA

Buy for Your Bustline

Big-busted gals look best in a tunic or wrap style that ties or knots in the front and doesn't have button-popping potential. Medium cups are prime for clean-lined designs with buttons that begin a few inches lower on the chest. Smaller busts can wear a tight button-down style or get a boost from tuxedo fronts, ruffles, and bust pockets. No matter what size you are, ruching is your friend. It can distract from a big bust when placed across the cups or maximize a small one by giving faux volume if positioned close to the main placket. Lafayette 148 New York is a great white shirt resource in petite, regular, and plus sizes (bloomingdales.com). J.Crew Three-Quarter-Sleeve Stretch Perfect Shirt is a good basic (jcrew.com), and New York & Company offers a number of styles that are easy work staples (nyandcompany.com).

Tszuj Do It . . . For truly fabulous, over-the-top-gorgeous white blouses, no one touches the perfection of Anne Fontaine. They are works of art and don't come cheap . . . but neither do Picassos. Check their Web site for seasonal sales and splurge on one, because these investment pieces will stay in style year after year (annefontaine.com).

Nip and Tuck

A trick I've used on many a fashion shoot is clipping in a white shirt from behind to define the waist. If you otherwise love the fit of your white shirt, have it tailored on either side to taper from the top of your rib cage to the slimmest point of your waist and gently flare back out to skim the top of your hip. Bring the pants or skirt you intend to wear with your top to the tailor, and make sure the adjustments made to the shirt can leave enough room to lay flat over a waistband or button fly without looking strained. For a slimming effect, look for shirts with darts, like Boss "Bashina" Stretch Poplin Shirt (nordstrom.com).

Have a Cool Collar

Don't commit the worst white-collar crime: a wimpy collar. You want something perky and stiff (well, don't we all?). A strong collar will frame your face, balance your frame, and create a prime backdrop to statement jewelry. Popping the collar (just pinch and glide up with your thumbs from the back base) gives it a crisp appearance that works anytime, anywhere. Think of white-shirt icon Carolina Herrera and her brilliant way of balancing a strong collar with a taffeta ball-gown-style skirt.

5. SKINNY BLACK PANTS

You might think cigarette pants make your legs look more like cigars, but let's be clear: In no way do you need to be skinny to wear skinny black pants. There is a pair for absolutely everyone and every shape. It's all in what you choose.

Look at Texture

Think in makeup terms and keep it matte, not shiny. More reflective fabrics and waxed finishes are fun for pencil legs but will highlight volume down south, while flatter finishes will make any lumps recede. Try a stretch wool or wool crepe fabric for fall/winter and a cotton blend for spring/summer.

Mind Your Midsection

High-waisted styles look chic but are tricky because they don't have the stretch to suck you in like high-waisted jeans can. That's why tummy pooches show more easily. Think about how your yoga pants have a wide crisscross panel that flattens any ab flab. Your goal is to replicate that sucked-in effect and steer clear of a muffin top with a one-and-a-half or two-inch waistband that sits just below your belly button.

Stick to Straight Leg

You can get away with a slight flare at the bottom, but a straight leg and pocket-free design gives a cleaner overall look. Elie Tahari Jenny Stretch Wool Pants and Eileen Fisher Plus Size Slim Ponte Pants are slimming options (both at saks.com). A black tuxedo stripe not only adds dressy flair but also an elongating detail too. Try 3.1 Phillip Lim Wool Tuxedo-Striped Trousers (saksoff5th.com).

Just Add Leather

Everyone should own a pair of wool trousers, but leather comes in at a close second. Look for a mid-waisted style with no back pockets and horizontal stitching above the knee. This little detail will help the leather fall straight, which gives you a leaner line instead of grabbing your knees and calves like a leather jegging would. Theory and Rag & Bone have a few fab versions (theory.com; rag-bone.com). Don't do half leather, half spandex styles—it's like buying a Porsche with cheap fabric seats. It's an all-or-nothing kind of thing.

6. FITTED BLAZER

Blazers add professional polish to the T-jeans-stiletto look like no other jacket can. A well-fitting blazer's structured front and lapel are designed to give you just enough of a triangle shape in your shoulders to minimize your waist, and enough downward angle to give your middle a torso-trimming look.

Copy Stella

No one cuts women's blazers better than Stella McCartney. The price point is high, but if you follow her lines, you'll be able to mimic the same sleek look with a more affordable brand, like Theory(theory.com), Tommy Hilfiger (usa.tommy.com), or H&M (hm.com/US). Check out stellamccartney.com for ideas (and peek on therealreal.com for consigned Stella blazers).

Love Your Lapel

Look for a slightly peaked lapel (when the notches go up), which balances the shoulders. Shawl-collared (or curved-lapel) blazers have a softer look that can be dressier. For bigger busts, a slimmer lapel gives a more streamlined look and will skim over your chest instead of sitting awkwardly.

Keep It Tight

Just like in tennis, don't go too long or too wide. Otherwise you're getting into boxy eighties territory. A blazer should be fitted across your shoulders without pulling. The ideal place for your blazer to fall is at the midline of your back jeans pockets to give your backside a tight, structured shape. You want to be able to button it just above your own belly button (go for a single-button style) so the blazer cuts in at the smallest part of your waist and skims your hips.

7. DENIM

Jeans are a wardrobe must-have, day and night, any season of the year. They're personal, they're forgiving, they're uncomplicated, and they go with just about everything. Here's how to be a denim-buying jeanious.

Keep It Simple

Ripped jeans are fun (I'm an occasional knee flasher myself), but if you're looking for a leg-lengthening look take you from day to night, go with a dark wash without fussy details. That means colors, patches, grommets, and artwork of Jerry Garcia are not on the agenda.

Size Down, Not Up

All jeans have a little give the more you wear them. Tough it out for the first three wears. When you find a pair that really works for you, buy them in multiple washes and colors.

Neg the Jegs

Jeggings might be comfy, but in my opinion they're a bit too lazy looking. Because they don't have internal structure due to the high rayon and polyester factor, they don't do your thighs or tush any favors. Jeans are best with a little stiffness that glides over—and doesn't cling—to any lumps 'n' bumps. The higher the percentage of cotton, the more structure you'll get . . . with a little bit of Spandex to stay fitted to your frame.

Go Mono

Avoid high-contrast stitching in white, gold, or other colors. The more monochromatic the thread looks with the jean itself, the more of a slimming, streamlined look you'll achieve. And they also look more modern and dressier—meaning you can wear them to many more places.

- -

BUTT *seriously* . . .

If you don't dry-clean, wash jeans in cold, inside out, and air dry. It's the best way to prevent fading and shrinkage.

- -

Hem the Gems

Each night before bed, I pray that I'll awake as Gigi Hadid. But since that hasn't come true for anyone but Gigi, we're all stuck hemming our jeans. Styles that are too long look sloppy (especially with a flared leg), and ones that are too ankle-y scream flood-watch alert. The perfect break will hit below your ankle. Bring your heels and boots when you have your pants hemmed, and remove and reuse the original hem stitching instead of having a fresh one made. It gives a cleaner, more authentic look.

Steal 'n' Splurge

White jeans may last you two seasons, tops, before they start looking yellow, so go with Uniqlo (uniqlo.com). Well-made dark denim will break in and last, so invest in the best. Brands worth the bucks are Paige denim, AG, Rag & Bone, Current/Elliott, and my favorite, the Citizens of Humanity Rocket High Rise Skinny Jean (all are available at major department stores). They're high quality and have great washes, and they comfortably conceal muffin tops and lengthen legs like magic.

---

casson confession: MY BLUE PERIOD

- -

Are you just as excited as I am that Sarah Jessica Parker is the new face (and booty) of Jordache Jeans? I remember watching Jordache commercials on channel 11 and singing along to the disco dancers, "You've got the look that's all together. Workin', playin'. Day or night!" And who can forget Brooke Shields and her iconic words, "You want to know what comes between me and my Calvins? Nothing."

I got my first pair of Calvins for Christmas in fourth grade, after seeing them on a classmate named Nancy Kalb. Nancy was the fashion plate of our school . . . and she didn't even go to our school! I said, "Mom, I'll have what she's having." After my denim dream came true, I remember insisting to mom that I must dry-clean my Calvins (at $1 a pop) to preserve the color (which, as opposed to my cashmere sweaters, I still do to this day). Then my growth spurt hit and they looked like the pedal pushers Rizzo wore in *Grease*. And I was way more Sandy! Puberty can be so cruel!

Like the perfect love or the perfect unbroken Parmesan cheese swizzle, it's hard to find the perfect pair of jeans. So if you spy them on someone else, ask for the brand and style. She'll be more flattered than annoyed. Everyone loves being a Nancy!

> *It's an old-fashioned idea that you must have a new dress for every occasion or party. Even if you have the money to do so, it isn't necessary. The modern approach is to change accessories.*
>
> EDITH HEAD

At the Governor's Ball After Party with *Will and Grace*'s Megan Mullally, after I accidentally de-blinged my borrowed watch at the Emmys.

carson confession: BLING A DING-DONG

Back when *Queer Eye* was first nominated for an Emmy, it was amazing how many people were kind enough to loan us chic things to wear to the ceremony. I remember Roberto Cavalli gave me the most beautiful tuxedo jacket with embroidered birds and gorgeous gold threading. Jacob the Jeweler gave me a gigantic watch—an iced-out Roly, if you will, with a spinning diamond bezel. It looked like the rim of a pimped-out car. I was nervous during the whole ceremony and was twisting the dial on the watch, hoping we would win. We lost that year . . . and I realized I'd lost something else. At the end of the ceremony I looked down to check what time it was, and the watch was there, but the diamond bezel was gone. I had been spinning it backward all night and unscrewing it. Sweet baby Jesus!

It was like $30,000—not the watch, just that *part* of the watch! And it was somewhere on the floor of the Shrine Auditorium! I was on the floor digging through candy wrappers and Susan Lucci's abandoned acceptance speeches, and of course I never found it. I went to security and told them my problem, and they were like, "Yeah, good luck with that." I had to take a polygraph test and sign an affidavit saying that I did indeed lose it and didn't steal it, so they could file an insurance claim. I don't know what the moral of this story is. Maybe it's "Don't twist your $30k diamond bezel the wrong way." Or maybe it's "Sometimes fake bling is better than the real thing." Think about times when you travel or have an important occasion. You don't want to feel like your accessories are a liability. Cubic zirconias look so good nowadays, no one can tell. So cut the cortisol and travel with your fabulous fake jewels.

Fifteen
TSZUJ-IT ACCESSORIES

When I worked at Ralph Lauren, one of the things Ralph said that I never forgot was, "The last thing you put on is the first thing people notice." Whatever that crowning-glory piece is, whether it's a scarf, a cardigan, a great bangle, or sunglasses, that one item is what people will see first. So the last thing you put on shouldn't be an after-thought—it should actually be the one you think the most about.

BLING

Delicate gold layering chains

Gold or textured cuff

Dangly earrings

Chunky statement necklace with beads or stones

Cocktail ring

BAGS

Neutral evening bag (raffia, python, leather)

Dark evening bag (leather, patent, satin, bejeweled)

Animal print clutch or baguette

Black structured daytime bag

Hobo purse in a neutral, like caramel, taupe, pebble, or moss (yes, consider army green a neutral)

BOOSTERS

Lightweight cotton scarf with a subtle graphic print

Brown leather belt with sleek rectangular buckle in silver or gold

Skinny black croc belt

Fedora

Oversize sunnies or aviators

Tszuj Do It... Spoil yourself at baublebar.com. Their Guest Bartender section showcases rotating designers' affordable statement jewelry that will elevate that crisp white shirt, LBD, or even a T-shirt and jeans.

marry, shag, kill

When you're wardrobe building, it's key to decide which items are long-term, one-season stands, or total losers. Which makes me wonder: If I was a velvet blazer, which category would George Clooney put me in?

MARRY	SHAG	KILL
Bags. Opt for one fabulous bag over three so-so ones. You can strike gold at an outlet or on sale—but look for signs of good craftsmanship, like real skins and leather, evenly spaced stitching, quality hardware, a nice lining, and tight interior corners.	**Bling.** Costume jewels aren't exactly cheap . . . even the cheap ones! I have a faux gold watch that turns my wrist black every time I wear it—but I still love it. Just remember that for five $250 bangles, you could invest in one beautiful gold piece and have it forever.	**Cheap denim.** Don't get seduced by the allure of $29.99 jeans; they'll just let you down with inferior construction and dye fading. Wait for a designer pair to go on sale.
Shoes. Unless you buy quality, they just look cheap and are an instant "tell" that you're cutting corners with style.	**Trendy tops.** Wear them to death all season until they literally deconstruct, then buy anew; you'll be sick of them anyway!	**Plastic and pleather.** Most items made with these materials won't "break in." They'll just break.
Belts. Don't skimp on a good belt. Go for real skins or genuine leather, plus great hardware that won't tarnish.	**Swimwear and sportswear.** It's hard enough to get through a season without even the best materials stretching or fading, so buy breathable fabrics that are just for the now.	**Designer Ts.** I cringe when I see T-shirts for $99. You can get away with basic tees from Gap, Zara, Hanes, or Fruit of the Loom (my nickname in college!).

BECOME YOUR own STYLIST

Speaking from experience, stylists often don't get face time with their clients before making clothing selections for them. That's why they rely on asking clients a list of questions first. Ask yourself the following to get a better picture of what your style is.

ASK YOURSELF:

What are my favorite colors?

Who are my favorite designers?

What are my go-to silhouettes (short skirt, relaxed fit, skinny jeans, roomy sweaters)?

Do I prefer patterns and brights to mono-chromatic and textures?

What is my favorite jeans brand?

Am I drawn to tailored handbags or funkier ones?

Do I go for sparkly embellishments or prefer the pared-down look?

What is my overall style (classic, preppy, boho, edgy, sporty, or a combination)?

carson confession: A RIVERS RUNS THROUGH IT

A few years ago, I had the good fortune of spending the day with Joan Rivers, who was such a joy. We were both guests on the Katie Couric show, and I was friends with Joan's stylist, who had kindly introduced us. Our dressing rooms were next to one another's, so I wound up having a fabulous girls gossip session with Joan and her daughter, Melissa. When I looked at the rack of Joan's potential outfits that her stylist had pulled for her to wear on air, something struck me: Everything was in harmony. Joan wasn't into bright colors and flashy patterns: It was all about embellishments, tones, and textures. Skirts, blouses, jackets, and pants were in ivory, black, and gold and were so easy to mix and match. Clearly, Joan knew what she liked and what "uniform" suited her best. And since all the pieces were indeed "going to the same party," any of them could be interchanged for an almost endless combination of looks.

The next time you have an important occasion coming up, think like a stylist and pull your favorite tops, bottoms, jackets, and dresses out and view them on your rolling rack a few days in advance. See what pieces can work together and what themes emerge, as if you were creating your on-air wardrobe. If you find yourself getting frustrated because your grouping is made of one-hit wonders that lack cohesiveness, now you know what to shop for.

WHO'S YOUR FASHION CRUSH?

Find out which style maven you're most in tune with, then follow my hints on maximizing that connection with your Twenty-five Easy Pieces and Fifteen Tszuj-It Accessories.

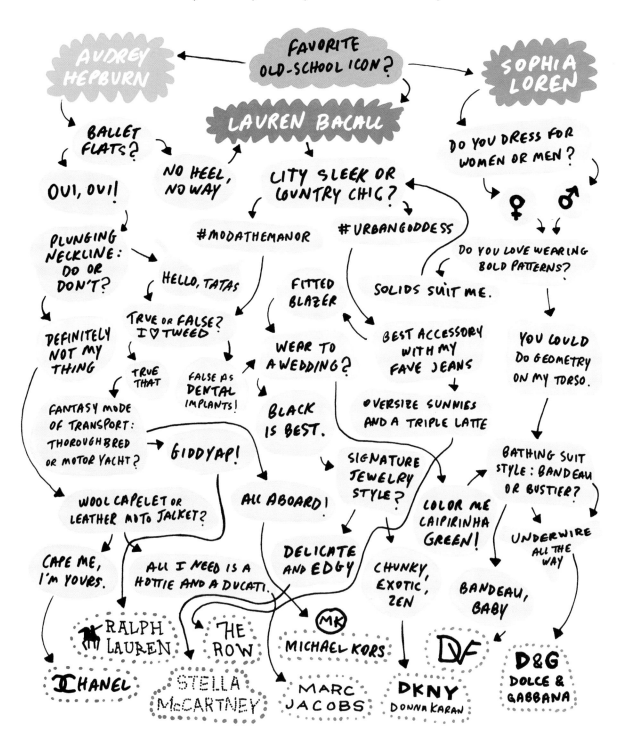

WHO'S YOUR FASHION CRUSH?

IF YOU CHOSE:	The look you love	Try these more budget-friendly brands instead.	Accent your wardrobe with designer details.
Chanel	Feminine details, structured yet ladylike pieces, delicate textures mixed with nubby fabrics, boatneck styles, cropped black pants	Alice and Olivia, Milly, Lela Rose, Tracy Reese, Rebecca Taylor	Add a boucle jacket (you can even find ones at Stein Mart) or a chain-strap baguette to your skinny black pants, flats, and printed blouse.
Ralph Lauren	Classic American style mixed with old-world glamour	Lauren Ralph Lauren, C. Wonder (now at QVC)	Add a faux-fur vest to your white jeans, black turtleneck, short brown boots, and big-buckle belt.
Stella McCartney	Sharp silhouettes with a dash of rock 'n' roll	Consigned Stella McCartney items on therealreal.com; CATHERINE Catherine Malandrino	Add a peplum or lacy top to your pencil skirt, nude pumps, animal-print clutch, and gold cuff.
The Row	Clean lines, structure, monochromatic color schemes	Theory, Vince., Current/Elliot, The Kooples	Add an asymmetric sweater to your skinny black pants, leather jacket, boots, and bold modern jewelry.

WHO'S YOUR FASHION CRUSH?

IF YOU CHOSE:	The look you love	Try these more budget-friendly brands instead.	Accent your wardrobe with designer details.
Marc Jacobs	Spunky and sassy items with a mod edge	Marc by Marc Jacobs, Forever 21, Zara	Add a lightweight military jacket to your dark denim jeans, tank, statement necklace, and flats.
Michael Kors	Jet-set wear with bohemian flair	MICHAEL Michael Kors, Tory Burch	Add a chambray shirt and aviators to your white jeans, gold cuff bracelet, and wedges.
Donna Karan	Flowy, Zen, monochromatic pieces that are oh, so comfortable	DKNY, Eileen Fisher, American Apparel	Add drawstring linen pants to your tank, cotton printed scarf, dangly earrings, and wedges.
Diane von Furstenberg	Sexy, flattering styles in bright colors and wear-anywhere fabrics	DVF, Trina Turk, Nicole Miller, Jones New York, INC International Concepts at Macy's	Add a colorful wrap dress, if yours is black or navy, to your nude heels, light clutch, and layering chains.
Dolce & Gabbana	Bodycon pieces in kaleidoscopic colors, or dramatic pieces in white or black	Clover Canyon, BCBG, ZAC Zac Posen	Add a corseted satin top to your dark denim jeans, blazer, strappy sandals, black clutch, and cocktail ring.

BUT CARSON, I Can't Shop FOR MYSELF!

I often hear the same worries coming from women I've transformed when it comes time for them to start shopping on their own for their Twenty-five Easy Pieces. Behold, some handy anxiety annihilators:

FASHION FEAR:
"Everything Looks Too Young for Me."
It's easy to talk yourself into thinking that you can't pull off certain styles of the moment—and maybe in certain iterations of that look, you can't. But that doesn't mean you have to ditch the trend completely.

SASSY SOLUTION:
Find a Streamlined Version
Keep looking and you'll find a grown-up version with built-in structure. My friend's seventy-one-year-old mother was going to a concert with her girlfriends and was tired of wearing boring black pants. For her birthday, she said, "Bring. It. On." and bought herself a pair of Rag & Bone brown leather pants that lifted her tush and sucked in her tummy. She paired them with cute boots and a navy top. Not only did she feel great, her girlfriends told her she had the body of a twenty-something. Look out, Selena Gomez.

FASHION FEAR:
"I Can't Wear White."
Many women shy away from buying clothing in white or ivory, especially on the bottom, and it's understandable why. I learned by working on TV that when you wear white, you glow a little bit. That extra glow can make you look fatter, quite honestly. You just need to be strategic about where you wear it.

SASSY SOLUTION:
Make White a Highlight
Don't ban the hue for good—simply use it strategically. Don't wear a tight ivory sweater that will emphasize your arms if they're your no-show zone; choose a crisp white shirt under a navy blazer instead. Instead of donning a solid white dress, go for a darker version with a subtle white pattern. If you have a big butt and are worried about white jeans, wear them with a long camel cardigan. Or make white a supporting player, like a white enamel bracelet and woven clutch.

FASHION FEAR:
"I'll Have to Return Everything I Buy Online."
It's not the worst thing in the world to slap a prepaid return label on a box, but the demoralizing part is not being able to figure out how to buy basics

when you can't touch or feel them, or gauge how they'll look on your body.

SASSY SOLUTION:
Size 'Em Up
When you're browsing online, look at the models and mannequins for style subtleties. Yes, they're 105 pounds and Amazonian height and sometimes made of plastic (just like some real models!), but get past that for a second. Does the fabric fall smoothly over the waist or cling to it? Does a dress cut too high into the upper arms, or does a sweater hit at the crook of the elbow? When you see enough outfits on the same form, you notice how different cuts, prints, and fabrics drape over the body differently and are universally more or less flattering. Think about the item's strengths and weaknesses, put your body into the equation, and only choose pieces that are guaranteed home runs. But don't beat yourself up if you strike out and have to put it back in the box. I do it, too.

- -

BUTT *seriously* . . .
Plug in one of your Twenty-five Easy Pieces, like "black cocktail dress" or a trendy item you're thinking about purchasing, to shopstyle.com. You'll see multiple versions of the same concept in the same color, which will help you eyeball which cuts are more flattering than others. The more subtleties you begin to process, the easier it will be to realize, *This is going to look amazing on me.*

- -

FASHION FEAR:
"I Just Don't Know How to Bargain-Shop."
I know it can be intimidating to set out with a particular budget and expect to acquire a trove of fabulous finds, but it is possible: I do it for a living!

SASSY SOLUTION:
Check out Chapter Four
Remember what basics you need in your wardrobe and give yourself enough time to go on the hunt for them. I'll teach you sneaky and savvy insider secrets that professional shoppers use to score seriously good merch—when to do it, where to do it, and how to save buckets of ducats.

4.

Being a
BARGAINISTA

Because when I shop, the world gets better.

REBECCA BLOOMWOOD,
CONFESSIONS OF A SHOPAHOLIC

ONCE THERE WAS A BOY WITH GOLDEN HAIR, bright blue eyes, and a fondness for doe-eyed Disney characters. Me! I didn't grow up in a castle or have two wicked stepbrothers, but I have a wicked wardrobe and get a wicked hangover from the occasional tequila and soda. Fresh out of college, I was offered a job with a nonprofit in the equestrian sector and hopped on a stagecoach called Bieber Tourways (no, it was not Justin's fan bus), bound for New York City. I would finally live in the big city! I was following my very own Yellow Brick Road, and its name was I-78.

What I didn't realize was that there was an evil force lurking. It was called rent. It gobbled up my paltry salary, leaving barely enough left over for ramen noodles, subway tokens, and Paula Abdul CDs. What was I, the poor young man, to wear? I wasn't about to look unfashionable. In the words of Frank Lloyd Wright, "Give me the luxuries of life and I will willingly do without the necessities!" I was prepared to go all-out Abe Lincoln and forgo electricity if it afforded me a cashmere cable-knit. Luckily, it didn't come to that. I've always been a bargain-shopper, and this divine gift is what saved me. As a boy of eighteen, I used to hop over to Reading, Pennsylvania, to buy XXL-size items from the children's Ralph Lauren outlet. They were the same as a men's small! That savvy skill would serve me well as a Manhattan newbie, as I acquired more and more Ralph Lauren merch from nearby outlet malls. It was my secret weapon.

One fateful day, I went to the gym. I didn't go there to exercise but to socialize in cute outfits (natch). This morning, it was slimming Black Watch–plaid track pants, a Ralph Lauren sweatshirt complete with Teddy Bear graphic holding a basketball, and the crowning accessory: a Ralph Lauren plaid basketball, which I casually cradled in the crook of my arm. It had been a free gift with an RL cologne purchase and probably fifteen coupons. I had no idea what a basketball was used for, but I knew it pulled my whole look together.

A typical Ralph day for me. You can overdress and occasionally underdress, but never overpay!

Lo and behold, a grand goddess appeared in the gym. She said, "Young man, you look like you should work for Ralph Lauren." What? *Moi*? "I agree!" I chirped. "Can you get me a job?" She waved her wand, and before long, I was an RL minion, working as the assistant to an assistant in the golf department. The first time I encountered King Ralph, it was in an elevator. He pointed at me and said, "Golf?" Thinking fast on my feet, I pointed back and said, "Billionaire?" I made the legend chuckle! It was like *The Devil Wears Prada*, but people were nice! N-I-C-E.

I learned a few things very quickly: I must dress exceptionally well at this job, noting that my coworkers would blow their entire salaries on pinstripe suits and pocket watches, cashmere ponchos and shearling coats (which was a killer even with the 30 percent employee discount). Ever watchful of my budget and fearful of one day becoming homeless, I insisted on hitting the outlet malls, sample sales, and squirreling away department store coupons like nuts for the winter. With care and cleverness, I managed to look as sharp as my colleagues. In fact, one day, Ralph sat in on a meeting at which the top brass were brainstorming looks for the spring collection. The team was stumped. What should the beautiful models wear for the upcoming shoot? Ralph glanced across the room at me and said, "Like what Carson has on." The harps played, the birds sang, and even after I left the enchanted land of Ralph Lauren, I never forgot this lesson: You can always look amazing on a budget. I've been bargain-shopping happily ever after.

I love the thrill of the hunt, and I must have channeled my straight male gene of punting footballs into hunting for bargains. As a stylist and professional shopper, much of my job is buying a billion different things and giving clients choices. I once got a letter from Saks saying I was buying and returning too much and I was on probation! On my Instagram, I call myself a retail enthusiast, because I'm literally in a store every single day.

Whether I'm on vacation and I'm checking out the local greats in little towns in Mexico or in Milan, or when I'm at home in Pennsylvania, I'm always going to Stein Mart and T.J.Maxx and Macy's so I'm aware of what's out there. That's more than I can ask you to do, but I think there is a power in window-shopping because you get a sense of the trends, and you open your eyes to things you didn't know existed, which can be a blessing and a curse. Oh, there's a new Trinity ring in platinum? Ignorance is bliss . . . especially when Pandora's box is Cartier Crimson or Tiffany Blue.

Don't get me wrong. I love a little luxury, and I'll carefully decide what's worth splurging on (more on that later). But the adventure of going to Target or Saks Off Fifth or Forever 21 and seeing all of these discounted designer deals, whether they're real or perceived, fills me with glee. Who doesn't want to know they scored something under market value?

carson confession: MY CINDERFELLA FANTASY

One of my favorite bargain glory moments happened at the cash register at Neiman Marcus Last Call outlet store. The woman ringing up my purchase asked if I'd like to sign up to get special e-notifications from the store. I reluctantly signed up, thinking, "Oh, great, that's the last thing I need—something more clogging up my e-mail." But wowzers, was I glad I did! I was e-mailed a coupon for 50 percent off of an item for one day only at the Neiman Marcus outlet in Camarillo, California. I printed it, went, and picked out a cotton V-neck T with a skull on it (remember when skulls were so in?).

As I was wandering, the heavens opened and I saw a ray of light shining down on a showcase filled with two perfect shoes: goatskin loafers in a buttery tan with russet accents and the most amazing heel. They whispered, "C'mon, try me, Carson. . . ." I gasped, "Could these be Tom Ford? Oh, they are!" I began frantically looking for a salesperson with a key to open up the vitrine so I could handle them, inhale the leather, and see if they were actually talking to me. The guy came and opened up the case, and I asked what size they are. "Forty-three," he said. Forty-three! I almost passed out. Tom Ford shoes are something that I never could buy because they are just so expensive—you could buy a used Kia for what they cost—but here was my bargain pair, and they fit to perfection! They were marked down from $3200 to $1600 to $800 to $650. Then I had my handy 50-percent-off coupon, which made them $325 . . . or $162.50 per foot!

I started jumping for joy, but then, just to pop my soul balloon, I squinted at the following words on the coupon: *save 50% on the LOWEST priced item in your basket.* So I have this skull T that's $12.99 and my pair of $600-plus shoes and shuffle to the register to check out. That was when the woman behind the register

you complete me.

said the magical words: "Which item would you like to use the coupon for?" I sheepishly said, "The shoes???" and she said, "Okay." I whipped my credit card out as fast as I could and bought them for $325. This was the closest brush with shoplifting I've had in my life! For fear that they'd chase me down for getting such a good deal, I started speed-walking out of the store into the parking lot, still thinking someone would stop me and say, "Excuse me, ma'am? We'd like you to come with us." I threw the key in the ignition of my rented Toyota Camry and sped over to the Barneys outlet in record time. There is a God!

QUIZ: DISCOVER YOUR BARGAIN-SHOPPING SPIRIT ANIMAL

Let's get started by ID'ing your bargain-shopping persona. The way you shop sales can reveal what makes you tick.

1. Your idea of a successful shopping experience is:

a. Prowling as many stores as possible from dawn till dusk.

b. Leisurely browsing your local boutique's sale rack.

c. Spending a power hour at a department store blowout.

d. Shopping on your laptop or phone while watching TV.

2. When are you most likely to shop a sale?

a. When are you *not*! You're always on watch!

b. You never plan; just stumble upon them.

c. When you get a store coupon in your mail-box or in-box.

d. When you see amazing promotions online.

3. How do you know an item is a worthy buy?

a. Your instinct tells you.

b. You think on it for a few days.

c. You ask a salesperson.

d. You comparison-shop.

4. What would make you a better bargain-shopper?

a. Not buying something just because it's a great deal.

b. Being quicker to act on coupons and sale dates.

c. Having the time and patience to do it.

d. Shopping outside of your go-to places.

5. Think about your last excursion to an outlet mall. You:

a. Didn't mind risking it and bought things without trying them on.

b. Felt overwhelmed all day by the all-you-can-eat outfit buffet.

c. Got exactly what was on your list and beat it out of there fast.

d. Bought less than expected, since you can always get deals online.

MOSTLY A'S: *Jaguar*

Aggressive with stamina to spare, you'll slink through any sale with confidence and speed. Outlets are your specialty. You don't question your natural instincts in making purchases and are a natural risk-taker. Who else would buy suede pants without trying them on first? Remember: When you get trigger-happy and start buying just because "it's on sale," you'll blow your wad on cheap items.

BUTT *seriously*...

Create a new e-mail account solely devoted to shopping. With your new account, all of your promotional e-mails won't clog your in-box and will go to one place, where you can keep everything organized.

MOSTLY B'S: *Turtle*

You'd rather slowly inch your way through a smaller shopping environment, where the inventory isn't overwhelming and items are curated for you. When you see a beautiful outfit displayed in a store, you're more likely to slip it on, then mull it over. If you love one store's aesthetic, get to know the manager and ask him or her to contact you when sales are going on and pull new pieces for you based on what's worked for you in the past.

MOSTLY C'S: *Hummingbird*

You're a practical shopper who places a high premium on time. You shop best in one-stop-shopping environments like department stores, from shapewear to formal wear. Your MO is to swoop in, cross items off your list at lightning speed, and fly outta there. Consider opening a discount-store card to the one place you gravitate to most so you can double down on sale periods and receive e-mail blasts on when to shop for the best value.

MOSTLY D'S: *Shark*

Analytical, you like to scan everything that's out there before you make your move, whether it's miles away or in cyberspace. Sometimes you browse for browsing's sake when you don't have an appetite for buying. This gives you perspective to know when a sale is just a sale or something worth biting into. Online shopping is a no-brainer for you; just don't make that your only mode.

MY TOP-TEN FAVE OUTLETS IN THE WORLD

Cabazon Outlets in Cabazon, California

Fashion Outlets of Chicago

Freeport Village Station, Maine

Space: Prada Outlet in Montevarchi, Italy

Las Vegas Premium Outlets

Twin Cities Premium Outlets in Eagan, Minnesota

Orlando Vineland Premium Outlets in Orlando, Florida

The Galleria, Houston, Texas

Woodbury Common Premium Outlets in Central Valley, New York

Tszuj Do It... Give your new shopping e-mail account a fun moniker to go with your retail alter ego. Mine is ShopsWithGoodCredit. It's my Native American name.

How to Survive OUTLET SHOPPING

Dig it or dread it, outlet shopping can be an amazing resource if you know how to work the system like a seasoned pro. Here's how to navigate an outlet without getting sticker shock—or seriously sapped.

PRINT COUPONS

A month before you plan to go, sign up for e-mail promotions so you're armed with coupons. Chances are if you visit the kiosk when you arrive, they'll give you a coupon of 10 percent off. This can be fabulous if you're already walking into a store with 30 percent off and can combine them for 40 percent off.

PRETEND YOU'RE AT DISNEYLAND

Literally mark off the places you want to go and what order will be most efficient so you don't get a bad case of outlet FOMO. I hit the largest stores first, like Neiman and Saks Off Fifth, because those big box outlets are the most tiring and are where you're going to get the most visual fatigue. There are a lot of things to look at, and you want to be fresh.

TIME IT RIGHT

Weekends are the worst time to hit an outlet, when you'll likely get stuck in a parking labyrinth, bump up against busloads of roller-suitcase-toting TOMs (tourists on a mission), and fight for dressing rooms. Fresh merchandise usually ships to outlets early to midweek, so Tuesdays and Wednesdays are your best bet.

- -

Tszuj Do It . . . Always ask if there are any additional discounts when you get to the register. Oh, and did you know that teacher and student discounts can be up to 20 percent?

- -

SAVE THE MO$T EXPEN$IVE FOR LAST

Smaller-footprint stores like Loro Piana or Prada have less square footage, more-limited merchandise, and a more-curated selection. I like to do those stops at the end not only because they're easier to shop but because they're still a splurge. By going to some of the bigger box stores first, you get a relative idea of what a deal is, so you can better gauge what you'll be shelling out at the chichi chains.

DO QUALITY CONTROL

Sometimes those one-of-a-kind samples that were made for production or for runway shows just happen to find their way to the outlet mall. Usually there's a little tag inside indicating that it's a sample. Those are the Willy Wonka golden tickets of outlet shopping; hold on and never let go! On the other hand, some clothing will be made just for outlets and never see retail stores, from polo shirts to dresses. Sometimes the simple reason is that they have extra yardage of a fabric. The items may not be as on-trend; they're more basic and the fabrics aren't as luxurious. Certain big-name designers do this, and I find that the price at the outlet doesn't warrant it because it's not that special. I would wait to go to Bloomingdale's for the real deal when they have a sale.

BE A QUICK-CHANGE ARTIST

Bring dress shoes in a pouch so you're able to have a good silhouette for trying on outfits, but make like a retiree in Fort Lauderdale and wear comfy shoes: nothing's more annoying than an outlet-induced blister. Also consider your outfit's flexibility. You may not have the opportunity to get into a fitting room if the store is packed. Would you be able to try clothing on over your own if the wait were forty-five minutes? Wear a nude tank so you're prepped. Jeans are a great base so you can try on belts and all-season wear.

AVOID BUYER'S REMORSE

I bought a Christmas gift for a friend from an outlet, and his Armani shirt is still sitting on my dining room table because it didn't fit. My friend is probably no longer speaking to me, because I've found no time to schlep back to the outlet to return it. A brand's nonoutlet store isn't going to take an outlet item as a return from you (trust me, I've tried; they basically look at you like you're covered in cold sores). It doesn't mean you should be scared to buy at outlets, but you need to either commit to the items you're buying and make them work through tailoring, or acknowledge that you may have some misses in that batch of hits.

TAKE THE TAILORING TEST

Speaking of tailoring, if you have to drastically alter it, put it back! There are certain things that are quick fixes in tailoring, like shortening a cuff or hemming shirts or pants; there are other things that just aren't worth it, like restructuring a jacket that involves changing the armholes and sleeves, or removing the zipper on a dress to accommodate a smaller waist. With the tailoring bill, something that used to be a deal is now costing you close to what you would have paid at retail. Or maybe even more.

DON'T GET DUPED BY DEALS

I once got caught up in the frenzy of buying a $7,500 Valentino wool cashmere topcoat at an outlet. (I know. To. Die. For.) It was marked down to $2400, then $1900, then $800—an undeniable deal. But unlike those amazing Tom Ford loafers, I do not need, nor do I ever really use or wear the coat that I just described. So I basically just threw $800 in *la toilette*. I got so mesmerized by the idea of this luxurious novelty item by a fabulous designer I admired that I really drank the Kool-Aid and bought something I didn't need and really couldn't afford. If it's out of your price range, even though it's a bargain, it's still going to cause you a lot of distress when your credit-card bill hits your mailbox or your in-box.

hands-free cross body purse

nude top for changing room ease

comfy shoes for store-hopping

Outlet Shopper's Outfit

Guilty AS CHARGED

Ever find yourself signing your credit-card slip, thinking, *This is a bad idea, but I so deserve this?* It's emotional overspending, and I fall victim, too. When I've just been dumped, I go out and buy something extravagant to make myself feel better as a distraction tactic. I usually feel better for the first five days as I walk around thinking, *Omigod, look at my new shoes, look at my crocodile belt. . . . I feel amazing.*

Then the credit-card bill comes and not only am I upset about being broken up with, I get my briefs in a twist about a bill I really don't want to pay. That splurge winds up being the emotional equivalent of downing an industrial-size tub of caramel corn: naughty at first, nauseating thereafter. Keep in mind that I'm the biggest shopping fan in the world. But if a purchase makes you feel stretched past your limits, it's just not worth it.

How do you know when the right buy has come along? Ask yourself these five questions:

CHECKLIST: ARE YOU SHOPPING FOR THE RIGHT REASONS?

1. Do I truly need it, or is it a Band-Aid? (It's okay to buy something simply to make yourself feel better, but make sure it stays within the limits of question five.)

2. Am I actually going to wear it? (There are items that are fabulous but you still don't wind up reaching for them in your closet. What's the point?)

3. Does it go with my existing wardrobe, or does it need a complete new wardrobe to work?

4. Is it going to make me feel fabulous—totally ready to put on and go?

5. Is it within my budget? I hate that word, but it's an essential to consider, and we all have one. But rejoice! Now, more than ever, you can look great on the cheap by mixing and matching.

Insider Tips FOR YOUR favorite MEGASTORES

There are so many big box and department stores competing for your shopping attention that it's easy to have your blinders on to even more savings. Here's a primer to maximize your experience without maxing out your credit card.

KOHL'S

They're really good at giving cash back, so if you're going to do a wardrobe refresh, this is the place. I've done many a makeover for TV, spent $400 and gotten $100 of "Kohl's Cash" back. I don't know about you, but I'll take free money any day! I love their Vera Wang collection for taking your evening wear up a notch.

CENTURY 21

This may be a great place for fast fashion (i.e., trendy basics), but it's also a gold mine for finding valuable sample clothing from runway collections and special productions. Century 21 will purchase them in bulk from a European jobber (someone who comes in and buys out old samples from a high-end brand like Altuzarra), which is how they make it onto the racks and into your lucky hands. They are only in the NYC metro area but worth the trip.

TARGET

Tar-jay is always rotating their designers to keep things fresh. It's kind of like playing fashion bingo: Will it be Missoni, Lilly Pulitzer, or Phillip Lim on the day you go? While the inventory is a little unpredictable, it can lead to fun and

affordable discoveries. Vow to spice it up and use those dollars for trendier designer items you stumble upon. You'll knock dollars off at the checkout counter by scanning your bar code from Cartwheel, Target's mobile app (cartwheel.target.com).

T.J.MAXX/MARSHALLS

Like Target, T.J.Maxx and Marshalls move through inventory superfast and are great if you're in need of variety. I know people who are addicted to stopping in on a weekly basis, just to see what new merch was brought in. You'll often find a big selection of Tory Burch, Prada, Gucci, and Ralph Lauren at T.J.'s, and clothing typically gets price-slashed on Wednesday mornings during restocking periods. One more reason to grab your latte and get there at opening time. Plus, they have a runway section with great high-end designers in certain key stores in ritzy areas. Ask around to find the one near you. Even if you pull off the tags at home thinking you want to keep an item but later change your mind, just take it back for store credit. How nice is that?

LORD & TAYLOR

There is so much inventory, how do you know where to begin? I recommend going to Lord & Taylor with a specific goal in mind, like looking for a dress for an upcoming wedding. Otherwise, you'll just get lost in a sea of fabric. If you take the time and have the patience, you will find it—and probably score a great deal. They frequently offer 20–40 percent off, and coupons are transferrable. Even if you don't have one, just ask the saleslady at the register, and chances are she'll whip one out of her drawer for you.

MACY'S

Macy's may not have the most Zen shopping environment, but if you're looking to seriously clean up, head to their One Day Sale, which happens one Saturday per month (*psst . . .* they also open it on Friday). Prepare to do a victory chant after scoring double and triple markdowns. Printing out their Wow! Pass online gives you an additional 20 percent off, which you can use on items whether you're shopping in-store or not. They also offer a point-accruing savings card called Plenti, but you don't need to talk yourself into getting one, given that there are always great promotions going on. Speaking of which, never buy something at Macy's full price unless you're madly in love with it. It'll get marked down in a matter of weeks.

BLOOMINGDALE'S

Besides having a great shoe and accessories selection and designer markdowns on everything from cashmere coats to swimwear, Bloomingdale's is big on keeping you in the loop (and getting your feedback). Make sure they know when your birthday is, because they've been known to mail out coupons after your first $100 purchase of the month. Joining Bloomie's Loyallist Program lets you earn points wherever you shop Bloomingdale's, even at their outlets. At five thousand points, you can redeem it for a gift card. If you spend $3,500 annually, you're bumped into their Top of the List level, which gives you perks like triple-points days, free shipping, and four points per dollar you spend—totally worth it.

- -

Tszuj Do It . . . Work those perks. If you have an eligible Amex card, you're entitled to a free membership for unlimited two-day free shipping through shoprunner.com, which can be used at Neiman Marcus, Lord & Taylor, and other stores.

- -

NORDSTROM

I kid you not: I have returned four-year-old sunglasses to Nordstrom (save those receipts!). A hinge broke, and they were willing to take them back and order me a new, updated pair. Talk about customer service that is *beyond*. Nordstrom Rack is a great resource for bargain finds, and while the regular store doesn't hit you over the head with sale promotions, their anniversary sales are strong (check out my calendar later in this chapter). My favorite new thing they offer is monthly Pop-In Shops (shop.nordstrom.com/pop) where you get access to "spec"-tacular brands like Warby Parker that you wouldn't normally see.

SAKS FIFTH AVENUE

Saks inventory really varies from store to store, ranging from fine to freakin' fabulous. I recommend spending more time traveling to mecca (i.e., a bigger Saks location) than wasting time at an outpost with slim pickings (in that case, you might as well be at Off Fifth instead). For online shopping, I like that you can actually stay within a designated price point using their handy widget, as long as you have willpower not to click out of your comfort zone. I always take advantage of their consolidation sale—both in stores and online—which happens in the summertime. Just read the fine print. When you buy those 60–70-percent-off items, returns are not always allowed. Sign up for Saks e-mail–only sales and you'll be privy to a percentage off your next purchase as well.

NEIMAN MARCUS

This department store is at the tippy-tippy-top of the food chain, and for good reason. Love the salespeople, the return policy, even the meticulous gift wrapping they did on a cashmere coat for my mother without my having to ask. It's called full service. And I like it. Plus, their designer merch is always on point . . . though price points are a tad steep. Your strategy: Shop NM's First Call, Last Call, and online clearance sales, which can be up to 75 percent off. It still isn't dirt cheap, but it's so worth it. Shoes (make that Choos?), handbags, and evening wear are satisfying steals.

- -

BUTT *seriously* . . .

With the Shop Your Way app (shopyourway.com) for Kmart, Sears, and Lands' End, you'll learn about deals and celeb fashion (did you know Nicki Minaj has her own line?) and get reviews and product info just by scanning the item with your phone. You can add your own comments, too.

- -

ARE YOU THERE, QVC?
It's Me, Margaret

TV networks like QVC and HSN are no longer the mysterious lands of porcelain dolls and embellished velour muumuus. Hipper designers, diverse inventory, and strong quality assurance make it a resource worth checking out. It's helpful to see items modeled for you in real time, as opposed to sifting through the racks or searching online, especially when it comes to jewelry. Try my tips for tube-shopping. . . .

GET BLASTED

Your first step should be signing up for the shopping networks' fashion insider's club e-mail blasts about what designers will be on and when to watch. Tune in to see what the item looks like on the models and hear the story of why that particular brand is worth your money. But before you dial, stick that trigger finger in a bowl of Cool Whip and keep reading.

HOP ONLINE

A brand's on-air selling is really a platform for their Web site. Instead of feeling compelled to "Call in now . . . there are only five hundred left!" you can peruse their entire collection and see what you really want. It's also a great way to shop if you need something specific. On Web sites you can search for "white capri pants" and see all their different styles and price points, as opposed to watching and waiting for nineteen hours.

SEEK OUT PROMOTION DAYS

When you do buy on the air, keep in mind that almost every network has a "fashion day" when they focus on selling all of their clothes and jewelry, and usually those days offer free shipping and returns. Put it in your calendar so you don't forget.

SIZE IT UP

Measure your bust, waist, and hips with their online tool, and you're set. After you do it the one time, you're golden. Many of the brands on the shopping channels come from the same manufacturer, so there isn't a lot of deviation in sizes. While there are different aesthetics and various price points, the fit is going to be very similar.

DON'T PAY ALL UP FRONT

Sometimes they'll offer an easy payment plan (think layaway, where you get the item instantly but pay a small monthly amount for a set number of months). It's a great way to try an item out, and if you don't like the item or it doesn't fit, or you just didn't enjoy the overall experience, you haven't made the full cash outlay.

TUNE IN DURING NOVEMBER AND DECEMBER

At holiday time, home shopping can be a great resource if you're looking to add eye-catching accessories to your holiday wardrobe without joining the stressed stampede at the mall. Clothing tends to be less prominent in these two months, though. While the networks will spend a lot of time on gift items and electronics during this time, hop over to the brand's Web site for fashion, because you'll often find slashed prices on all that end-of-year inventory that isn't getting airtime.

Tszuj Do It... Play around on trendme. net with their "dressing room" tool listed under their Create! tab. Pretend you're on *Project Runway* and that you will get a cash prize for best outfit in under five minutes. You'll surprise yourself with how creative you can be—which will give you confidence to do the same thing in an actual dressing room.

BUTT *seriously* ...

If you haven't heard of retailmenot.com, check out this online coupon aggregator. You'll become addicted to looking for online and in-store deals. You'll see the same deals on a store's Web site, but this site lets you know where to look first.

Buy-Curious?
THE FOUR HOTTEST MONTHS to Shop

Squelch that back-to-school itch or spring fashion fever in favor of more strategic shopping times. I'm giving you a year-round calendar, and if you can manage to do the bulk of your buying during some specific windows, you'll have more dough to spend overall.

JANUARY

January 2 is my big shopping day. During the holidays, you're not buying for yourself, and then Christmas comes and you might get a little cash in your stocking (or items you might need to trek back to the mall to return). By the time January rolls around, it's time to focus on reinvention. Ralph Lauren always marks down its winter inventory online, along with other major brands, like Victoria's Secret (show up the first day if you want matching sets; don't ask me how I know that). Even major department stores, like Neiman Marcus, will have an amazing shoe sale, trying to get rid of their holiday and fall merchandise to make way for their first delivery of spring, which comes in February. January is a great time to pick up things that you can wear now.

JULY

Around our country's birthday, billions of fireworks go off . . . in my head, because it's time to shop. Department and big box stores really start slashing their summer inventory this month, making it a prime time to stock up for next year. Who cares if you only have another few days to wear it; think big picture. From Walmart to Amazon, you can do some serious damage in this sale-centric month, but feel okay about it because the deals were just that good.

AUGUST

If sale items from July don't move, they'll get knocked down even further, in addition to pre–Labor Day sales that you can really work to your advantage. Plus, in at least sixteen states, you'll enjoy select tax-free days during the first two weeks of August. There's usually a spending cap, so choose wisely. I always splurge on footwear if I can.

NOVEMBER

Black Friday is more about door-buster sales for electronics, and I don't really get in on the madness (I'd rather make Martha Stewart papier-mâché turkeys and watch a *House Hunters International* marathon). My secret to optimizing Black Friday is hitting outlet malls on the Wednesday night before Thanksgiving. A lot of sales start early, but only the truly plugged in know that—which now includes you. You're welcome.

As for Cyber Monday, you're probably already signed up on all the e-mail lists of retailers you regularly shop, but also get on the more high-end brands that you normally don't, so you can take advantage of deals. I stay up late Sunday night to get the best grabs at 12:01. If you download the shopkick.com app, you'll get reward points to use at stores like Old Navy, Target, and Macy's after buying enough items.

YOUR bargain-shopping CALENDAR

JANUARY 2: Your major shopping and returns day; during the first week, white sales on winter clothing begin.

FEBRUARY: Neiman Marcus Last Call Sale

MARCH 17: St. Paddy's Day: costume emeralds or kelly-green stilettos, please!

APRIL 15: Tax Day = retail therapy at vintage/consignment shops with peak inventory

MAY 15: Nordstrom Half Yearly Sale; MAY 30: Memorial Day sales—Get to the outlets early!

JUNE 3: Victoria's Secret Semi-Annual Sale

JULY 4: Fourth of July sales, plus the biggest anniversary sales of the year at almost all department and big box stores and online; JULY 15: Amazon Prime Day sale

AUGUST: Tax-free shopping days during the first two weeks! AUGUST 31: Labor Day sales start early

AUGUST 15: Time to buy my back-to-school Louboutins!

SEPTEMBER 2, 3, 4: Labor Day sales for end-of-summer clearance

OCTOBER 10: Columbus Day sales and prime time to buy jeans in the wake of September's back-to-school frenzy

NOVEMBER: Nordstrom Half Yearly Sale for Women; NOVEMBER 23: pre–Black Friday sales; NOVEMBER 28: Cyber Monday

DECEMBER 26: Day one of on-sale clothing (and the best selection) through January; Barneys Winter Clearance Sale

FLASH SALES 411

There's something so *Amazing Race*-y about a flash sale—a ticking clock and scarcity creates a giddy journey through a site, where you really feel like you've won Olympic gold when you nab the last item left. But they can also make you impulse buy if you aren't careful. Here are ten savvy tips so you don't become flash-sale roadkill.

FAB FLASH SALE SITES

belleandclive.com

gilt.com

hautelook.com

ideel.com

myhabit.com

ruelala.com

therealreal.com

GAIN VIP ACCESS

On The RealReal, it's worth the extra five bucks per month to become a First Look Member, where you'll have access to sales a full twenty-four hours before everyone else. Gilt has a similar structure with a free rewards program that allows you to view sales up to thirty minutes before they go live for everyone else. I look at this as the real "flash" element of the sale—privileged access to the best of the best.

BE THE BLACK SHEEP

There is usually one major sale featured most prominently, with others just below it. Click through the other sales first. Why? Everyone is storming the featured sale (and realizing everything is "sold" or "on hold" and potentially slowing it down) while you, smartie, have open season on choice items in the other sales.

COMPARISON-SHOP

You scored a coveted item in your cart. Hooray. Now find out if it's really a deal. Google and search the item on department store sites and on shopstyle.com to price it out against all the retailers that carry it. Who made you so smart?

GO ALL IN

If you're not sure about an item, throw it in your cart anyway to buy yourself time before the clock runs out. Don't feel guilty for hoarding items while you're contemplating purchasing them. If you release them, you've effectively driven up their value! Case in point: How many times have you seen that an item is "on hold" for another person and lusted for it even more?

BE RUTHLESS

If there's an item you love on hold for someone else, open a new window with the "on hold" item and continually hit the refresh button. If she doesn't hit "buy," you'll be the first to nab it once it becomes available. If you're about to lose an item, wait ten seconds until it's about to disappear from your cart, type a descriptive search (like "Valentino grommet shoe") in the search box, and hit the refresh button when the clock has two seconds left. Back together again!

PLAN AHEAD

If you're a crazed multitasker like I am, you can set reminders for upcoming days featuring designers you're interested in. For example, Rue La La's iPad and iPhone app (also available for the Apple watch) offer push notifications for events like their Happy Hour sale and daily boutique openings.

DON'T GET SIZEHEIMERS

You see a must-have item you love in a size 8 or 12, but you're a tried-and-true 10. Or you know you're bottom heavy, but that pencil skirt with no stretch is calling your name. Don't go there . . . unless you love visiting the UPS return-shipping department.

PLAY FAVORITES

If your iPad malfunctions (the horror!) and everything disappears from your cart, which item would you remember to add back first? Close your eyes, have a deep spiritual moment, and ponder it. That's the one piece you should buy.

HIT THE PAUSE BUTTON

It's easy to get sucked in and pressured to purchase at lightning speed when you know there's "only one left." But some boutiques stay open for three hours, others for weeks, and there will always be another. Also, keep in mind that just because the sale is over doesn't mean the merch isn't still in the system. There are easy tricks to access past sales on some sites by doing a backward search by typing in the designer's name.

- -

BUTT *seriously* . . .

Beef up your designer intel. The Fix (myhabitfix .com) has a Designer Directory with blurbs on major designers offered on the site. It's a great way to get a crash course on who's who.

- -

BE AN OPPORTUNIST

Every site has a different ways to save. For example, on Rue La La and Gilt, paying an upfront $9.95 shipping fee gives you free shipping for thirty days, so it's wise to plan ahead for more buys that month. Other sites may charge you less shipping per item when you purchase multiple items. Take a good ten minutes to read through the site before you start shopping. There are almost always promotions for 20 percent off, and site credits from $10 to $25 for you (and in the case of Belle & Clive, for you both) when any friend you refer to the site makes a purchase.

GUARANTEE MANY HAPPY RETURNS

Before you buy, know the rules of returning. Will a label be sent to you? Does the tag need to stay on, or does the item need to be in its original packaging? Will shipping costs be deducted, and if you don't want the deduction, can you be rewarded in site credit or points to use elsewhere? Most sites allow returns minus a shipping charge, but some, like Gilt, are often final sale and non-returnable. On The RealReal, you can reconsign anything you've bought from them as long as it's in good condition. Typically you'll get two weeks to process a return, but on HauteLook, you have ninety days to return items to Nordstrom Rack, since the site is owned by Nordstrom.

four.sites WITH serious MOJO

Depending on what you're shopping for, these online destinations dish out great products at a discount. Which one suits you best?

FOR THE NO-FRILLS DEAL FINDER
Bluefly

From Super Sundays (think 80 percent off clearance) to their curated boutiques that span everything from activewear to shapewear to formal wear, bluefly.com delivers. Their clean Web design is super-easy to navigate, and their men's section is strong (because, hello, while your style quotient is rising, he needs to up his game). If you want a one-stop shop but don't like dealing with sites that feel too crammed with inventory, this is a good place to start. Pick a few boutiques to begin with to help drill down your options.

FOR THE SWEET SENTIMENTALIST
ModCloth

Besides its darling retro feel (think Betty Draper meets Taylor Swift) and wallet-friendly prices, my favorite thing about modcloth.com is their

Style Gallery uploaded by real women (click the "Outfit Photos" tab). Treat these galleries like a truth-telling mirror. If you notice that most women in the gallery seem to have large busts and you don't, you won't be surprised if you order the dress and the top is gaping (that's code for "buy and regret it"). Pinpoint which woman you most resemble shapewise. Say you have a little more party going on around your middle. How do curvier girls look in the item? If the answer's smokin', give yourself the green light. Galleries like these can also give you clues as to what skin tones look best with certain colors (i.e., should you buy the same dress in black or red?), and how to accessorize with shoes, jewelry, and bags.

FOR THE TRENDISTA
Shopbop

I think of shopbop.com as having a little something for everyone. Their range of designers is like a bento box of yummy options from well-known designers (Halston Heritage, Puma) alongside names you may never have heard of (Haus Alkire and Peixoto, anyone?). I love browsing through their lookbooks that correspond to calendar days of the month. Start there for inspiration with no expectations for buying, and just see what moves you. Then head over to the sale section, which is further divided by "percentage off," and put that aesthetic to work.

FOR THE SLEEK SOPHISTICATE
Yoox

Imagine going shopping all over the world, from the Côte d' Azur to Shanghai to the Grand Canyon, and sneaking in a few deals while you're at it. That's what it feels like to shop yoox.com. Most of the products are sent over from Italy, but the shipping costs aren't crazy (under $10.00 for standard shipping). Not everything is affordable—in fact, many things are not—but you can still find bargains on high-quality merch if you go straight to the sale section and stay there. I don't always sign up for promotions, but it pays to do it at myoox.com to get access to restricted areas on the site and info on upcoming deals.

BUTT *seriously . . .*

Some sites like shopbop.com allow you to use your Amazon Prime account for free two-day shipping, which is a major saving strategy if you're a frequent online shopper.

Now that you know the ins and outs of stealth shopping, it's time to step up your wardrobe game plan for all the fabulous, random, complicated, and outrageous occasions in your life. I'm talking everything from therapy sessions to game-show appearances to cruise-ship rock concerts (leather and tats and Bret Michaels, oh, my!). Because I happen to love being inappropriate . . . as long as you're dressed appropriately.

5.

WHO, What, WEAR

Dressing well is a form of good manners.

TOM FORD

YOU'RE LATE. YOU'RE TIRED. YOU'RE OVER it. You don't have time to Google "Leggings office appropriate?" or "Wear ivory to a wedding?" And then there's the question of what to wear for date nights, cross-country flights, and meetings with your shaman guru. You may not have the time or the energy to strategically plan for the occasion, so you quickly reach for your safe (that's code for "boring") standbys. Where's the joy in dressing if you always take the conventional route? To put a spin on my favorite interview question from *Inside the Actors Studio,* you don't want to enter the pearly gates and have God sigh, "Really, black yoga pants *again*?"

There used to be a time when wearing jeans on an airplane was considered gauche, but the world has loosened up and almost everything is fashionably possible. It's not about having the biggest budget or the smallest waistline. The key is dressing right for the right moments. Just as every Miley Cyrus tongue selfie has its own unique meaning, every life scenario has its sartorial counterpart—and gives you a fun excuse to get creative. Think of it as dressing up for your audience while still feeling

comfortable and "you." Who do you want to be today? What persona do you want to project in your surroundings? In case you're curious, today at brunch I'm aiming for international playboy on the Riviera, and tomorrow at a work meeting it will be "tweedy professor in the West Village" with tortoiseshell glasses and distressed jeans.

I once stumbled upon this Pinterest quote and it's stuck with me ever since: "Dress like you're going somewhere better later." Ever notice that others treat you with a little more sparkle on days that you've put some real attention into your outfit, even subconsciously? They're thankful you made the effort. Plus, you probably projected a happier, more receptive persona when you added a few pieces that made you glow. The whole act is self-perpetuating: The more attention you give to wearing the right thing at the right time, the more confident you look and feel. And I'm not just talking about dressing up. We live in a dressed-down society, so it's key to nail your casual wear so it truly expresses you and your style.

I'll give you an example of *not* nailing it: When I played the role of Man in Chair in the Broadway play *The Drowsy Chaperone*, I spent most of my days in baggy russet corduroy pants, an oversize olive-green Mr. Rogers cardigan over a thick Fair Isle sweater and a flannel button-down underneath. *It's just a costume!* I'd remind myself as I'd wander around town on my coffee break, but I couldn't help but feel like a total schlub. The low point was when someone stopped me in Starbucks to say he owned my same clunky two-tone hiking boots. I was like, "Um, yeah, thanks." Where's a brown paper bag when you need one?

This is my "Broad way" of saying there's a certain finesse to donning casual wear. The more casual the item, the more structure and polish you need to counterbalance the frump factor. A great place to start our little exercise in cultivating casual chic is in the world of athleisure.

BUT *seriously* . . .

Comfort clothes are great, but like comfort food, you don't want to get so hooked you don't recognize yourself anymore. Work from home? Ban sweats and actually get dressed in the morning, even if that means a cute top, earrings, Lululemons, and some lipstick.

Not my best look.

athleisure A TO Z

I won't lie: It took me a while to embrace the fact that athleisure is now outselling denim. But since we're spending so much more time Zumba-ing, Flywheeling, Cross-Fitting, Pure Barre-ing, SoulCycling, and Yogalates-ing—or if you're me, just pretending I know what any of those things are—it's only fitting that workout wear influences our daily wardrobe. The trick is to make your look a little more street and a little less gym.

BRAND: Sweaty Betty (sweatybetty.com)
Style MO: Hip and colorful with figure-flattering power
Best Bets: If you'd rather toss on a cute sweater and take the emphasis off of your lower half, try their Uttanasana Yoga Pants. They have a wider leg from mid-thigh to ankle, a roll-down waist, and come in three leg lengths that suit Lil' Kims and Uma Thurmans alike. Their Optimal Training Hoody is so flattering for the torso and upper arms that you can get away with at least fifty fewer sit-ups and two more cupcakes per week.
Perfect for Postworkout... Anything. Their Vinyasa Yoga Capris have flirty little side ties and ruching that contours your calves and look cute with flip-flops.

BRAND: Lululemon (lululemon.com)
Style MO: Sassy, simple, well-structured basics
Best Bet: What I like about Lulu's Pleat to Street Hoodie is its roomy bell shape that doesn't scream "gym." Another winner is their Vinyasa Scarf, which you can toss over a simple top. Swap out your sneaks for metallic ballet flats and you won't look like you just spent the last hour om-ing.
Perfect for Postworkout... TED talks. Did you know a number of their jackets and hoodies have media pockets with a cord exit?

"We look too cute to shower. Wine bar?"

- -

BUTT *seriously*...

A required athleisure accessory is a sporty statement bag. I like a quilted MZ Wallace tote (mzwallace.com) for the classic woman and ANDI bags (theandibrand.com) for edgier femmes.

- -

BRAND: Fabletics (fabletics.com)
Style MO: Kate Hudson's fab fitness line
Best Bet: It's easy to dress up a sweaty tank with their cotton-viscose Austin Wrap in Cloud Nine. It has a pretty drape and I like that it can be styled different ways. Add a long tassel necklace, a pair of jeans, and you're done. You'll have the dough to do so because the price points here are very user-friendly. Becoming a Fabletics VIP member means discounts on full outfits starting at $49.95. Each month, stylists will send personalized recos to you.
Perfect for Postworkout . . . shellac manis (consider the thumb hole), Starbucks infusions, book club meetings, and long walks with Bruno, who might be your dog, your soul mate, your personal trainer . . . or all three.

BRAND: Anatomie (anatomie.com)
Style MO: For the "jet-sweater" (i.e., a jet-setter who loves to sweat)
Best Bet: Browse their online outlet to score deals, like the body-contouring Madonna pant, lace and mesh long-sleeve Ts, or motorcycle-chic jackets with quilted details. These pieces are so well tailored, you'll be reaching for them on non-workout days. Bonus: Knit fabrication packs so well. No wrinkles—just pop on and go.
Perfect for Postworkout . . . lunches with girlfriends, a casual-dress day at work, hopping a flight and feeling jaunty enough to order cabernet sauvignon with your Pringles.

- -

Tszuj Do It . . . Get a crazy-sexy workout bra. It'll be your little secret—or not. Coobie makes killer sports bras in solids, as well as post-workout styles in camo and tie-dye that look adorbs peeking out from under a V-neck. And seriously, how cute is the name? (shopcoobie.com)

- -

BRAND: Under Armour (underarmour.com)
Style MO: Sporty to the max
Best Bet: I love their Women's UA Studio Wrap that comes in gray, green, and black. It's a cozy topper for cold days and has a flattering waterfall front. While I'm not exactly the rah-rah type, if you're dying to wear your alma mater's sports team (or just a team you admire) across your chest, their French Terry Popover is a slimmer version of your typical hoodie. Holy Toledo Rockets!
Perfect for Postworkout . . . after-school sports runs, standing in line at the bank, dry-cleaners, or corner pub when you want people to ask you about Notre Dame football.

BRAND: Pam & Gela (pamandgela.com)
Style MO: If Debby Harry or Chrissie Hynde were gym rats
Best Bet: Swap out your sweaty workout top for one of their Henley Ts, top it with bold jewelry, and you're good to go. From leather track pants to off-the-shoulder sweaters, these pieces make a statement without trying too hard.

Since this brand is from the makers of Juicy Couture, you know you're getting comfort with your edge. *Psst . . .* Gela is married to John Taylor of Duran Duran—so make like Rio and start dancing on the sand . . . or supermarket linoleum.
Perfect for Postworkout . . . therapy sessions (they have awesome graphic Ts with sayings like I'M NOT SORRY for your shrink to decode), a rock concert, or casual date night.

- -

BUTT *seriously* . . .
Wearing the wrong underwear can cramp your yoga-pant style. The nylon and spandex thong from empoweredbyyou.com will look invisible so you can look tush-tacular. Plus, you're supporting their amazing microfinance campaign!

- -

CARPOOL COUTURE 101

See that woman in her SUV pretending to yak into her cell while jerking her neck to stare at you? Yes, she's checking you out. Here's how to upgrade your threads.

Full Speed Ahead	Back It Up
Rock-star skinny cords or plus-size rock-star boot-cut cords (oldnavy.com) with a suede bootie.	Relaxed-fit cords (you know, the wide-wale ones that add five pounds and give you a diaper butt) with sneakers or Ughhs. I meant Uggs.
Slouchy denim terry track pant (pamandgela .com). You get the comfiness of sweats with streamlined cool.	Traditional baggy sweats. I know they're snuggly, but so is back hair, which I wouldn't recommend wearing either.
Zara's body-fit leggings with a wide waistband (zara.com). Wear them with a tush-skimming sweater or a simple T and jean jacket.	PJs. My friend Kat (I'm using a fake name to protect the innocent) was once pulled from her car into a surprise "parent-teacher conference" in flannel drawstrings.
Lightweight Vince cashmere cardigan (vince.com) that works with black leggings and skinny jeans.	Oversize fisherman's sweater. (Do you really want people to ask you if you're expecting?)
Slim tubular down vest from Uniqlo (uniqlo.com) or J.Crew (jcrew.com) that is weatherproof for drizzly days.	Giant puffer coat. Besides uncomfortable wheel turning, the Michelin Woman look can be scary.
Oversize scarf by ASOS (asos.com).	Throw blanket from couch, plaid picnic blanket.
Sleek boots, canvas slip-ons, trainers, ballet flats.	Bunny slippers, Reeboks, Birkenstocks.
Boyfriend jeans from Madewell (madewell. com), Levi's (levis.com), or, for a splurge, Current/Elliott (currentelliott.com).	Your boyfriend's actual jeans. I know you're in a rush and they are semiclean, but they just don't cut it. Especially with a NASCAR belt.
Baseball cap.	Shower cap.

QUIZ: DO YOU DRESS N.Y. OR L.A.?

The details in casual wear on the East and West Coasts are as different as Biggie and Tupac. Even if you live far away from either, it's fun to see where your style falls on the map.

1. Your everyday watch is:
   a. A sporty style with an oversize face that you stack with bracelets
   b. A classic silver or gold timepiece. It's money, honey.

2. The jewelry style you gravitate most to is:
   a. Diamond studs, an elegant cuff, or statement necklace
   b. Ear jackets or dangly styles with layering necklaces

3. What are your go-to daytime shoes
   a. Kitten heels
   b. Leather sandals

4. Your daytime accessories are:
   a. Aviators or wayfarers
   b. Oversize black frames

5. You feel the most "you" in a:
   a. Pencil skirt and stilettos
   b. Flowy sundress and wedges

6. What's your go-to shirt?
   a. Crisp white fitted button-down
   b. Relaxed-fit faded denim

7. Your everyday bag is:
   a. Structured leather
   b. Slouchy suede

8. On a casual day you'd pair skinny jeans with:
   a. Ballet flats (summer) and black slender boots (winter)
   b. Chuck Taylors (summer) and lace-up booties (winter)

9. On crisp days, your likeliest top layer is:
   a. Leather jacket
   b. Trench coat

10. Your go-to hat is:
   a. Baseball cap or wool beanie
   b. Cowboy or straw fedora

KEY: 1. a. LA, b. NY; 2. a. NY, b. LA; 3. a. NY, b. LA; 4. a. LA, b. NY; 5. a. NY, b. LA; 6. a. NY, b. LA; 7. a. NY, b. LA; 8. a. NY, b. LA; 9. a. LA, b. NY; 10. a. NY, b. LA

IF YOU SCORED SIX OR MORE NY's

You have a refined, elegant sensibility, preferring classic to trendy. You want people to take you seriously, and, darling, they do! Loosen up once in a while with a faded T or fringed hobo bag that says, "I *can* find my way off the island!"

IF YOU SCORED SIX OR MORE LA's

Laid-back sexy is your vibe. You prefer items that don't look like you're trying too hard, and as long as they aren't *too* casual, they transition well from work to play. Next up: power-lunching at the Ivy on Robertson. Order the Lobster Cobb!

IF YOU SCORED HALF AND HALF

You have bicoastal style, baby. Some days you feel beachy bohemian, and others, *Breakfast at Tiffany's* timeless. The key item that bridges both styles: a great pair of leather pants that capture East Coast chic and California cool all in one.

PACKING *tricks* FROM A RED-EYE WHIZ

Speaking of the N.Y.–L.A. divide, I travel between coasts so frequently, I guess you could say I'm not a Virgin anymore. (Though I do still get excited by said airline's good lighting, yummy snacks, and bizarre Swedish documentaries about boiling wool.) Here's what I've learned while scoring frequent-flier miles:

HAVE AN AGENDA

I used to pack everything, à la, *There might be a maharaja party; better bring my bedazzled turban!* Now I actually write down every lunch, dinner, awards ceremony, horse show, and work activity I'll attend, then pack only one option for each occasion. No choices, no extra weight. Like making room for a good meal, I'd rather my suitcase stay lean and put on weight from a shopping spree in my destination city. Don't even get me started on duty-free binges.

PACK YOUR GREATEST HITS

I always Google the weather when packing and assemble my hit list from there. Mine is often a white button-down, a blazer, jeans, and a black suit. Don't take a lot of fashion risks when you're packing: Your hits should simply be clothing you always feel good wearing. Spice it up with accessories: the hat, the scarf, the glasses, the sandals.

STAY IN SHAPE

Besides a deep-conditioner explosion, there's nothing worse than a mashed shoe when you go to open your bag. Help dent-prone items hold their shape (this goes for purses, too) by stuffing them with socks and underwear. I don't stuff my bras, though.

FOLD FABULOUSLY

Who has time for layering delicate tissue between garments? Sure wish I did, though! The next best thing is folding your sweaters and long-sleeve shirts better than a Gap employee: Lay clothing facedown and take each arm across (like a straightjacket . . . which I know absolutely nothing about). Fold each half vertically into the center, fold in half horizontally, and flip. Caveat: With items that crease easily, like linen and rayon, I have better luck sushi-rolling them.

BE COMFORTABLY CHIC

On the roulette wheel of fabulous flight mates, I'm usually seated beside one of three types: entertainment executive, rock 'n' roller, or Aussie en route to New York. My last flight involved category three, and her name was Heather, or as she introduced herself, "Hith-AH." She wore an ivory cashmere sweater, a white enamel Hermès bracelet, and for a nonjeans surprise, ticking stripe, high-waisted dungarees and rugged taupe booties. She incorporated a hint of the unexpected, but was still totally together. Or should I say, "togith-AH."

FOLLOW THE RULE OF THREE

As in, three pairs of shoes. If you can't do it, don't go over four. Think: a walk-anywhere pair, nighttime heels, flip-flops for swimming or spa-ing, and, depending on the season and locale, cross-trainers, flats, or boots. Another space-saving tip is to wear your boots on the plane, not pack them. Socks will save your feet on the dirty security-line floor and keep your tootsies warm en route. Just be sure to have flip-flops in your carry-on bag for a quick change if you're headed to a warm location, plus enough space to tuck in your boots (dump your *Vogue* and *Bazaar).* I've often seen people get out of snow-covered taxis at NYC airports in boots and arrive in St. Barts looking pretty ridic.

- -

BUTT *seriously . . .*

Navigate the airport in style so you still look cute while you're running between terminals. I recommend a rubber-bottomed ballet flat with supportive padding, like the Cole Haan Air Bacara (colehaan.com), which easily squishes into a purse if you switch to sandals or boots in your destination city.

- -

The only thing that separates us from the animals is our ability to accessorize.

**CLAIREE BELCHER,
*STEEL MAGNOLIAS***

- -

Tszuj Do It . . .

Cultivate statement luggage like an international woman of mystery! I love the bright, sporty designs of the Corroon roller case (corroon.com) that stand out on a crowded carousel. Its lining features the swallow, a symbol of a safe journey home, which seamen in the British Royal Navy tattooed on their bodies (ooh, my wings are flapping).

- -

YOUR AIRPLANE SURVIVAL KIT

Sometimes a little luxe goes a long way:

- **Bose headphones and backup AAA batteries**
- **Cashmere scarf or wrap (go oversize to double as a blanket or DIY pillow)**
- **Kiehl's 2.5-oz Ultimate Strength Hand Salve**
- **Dang coconut chips, because, dang, they're good**
- **Kindle loaded with *Champagne Supernovas* and *I'll Drink to That***
- **Elemis Pro-Collagen Hydra-Gel Eye Mask**
- **Lavender-scented EO Hand-Cleansing Wipes**
- **Ambien ("Am" just "bein'" honest!)**
- **Selfies with Bobby, my cute steward**
- **Tom Ford Hydrating Lip Balm**

carson confession: SEARCHING FOR DOLCE & GABBANA

Back when I worked at Ralph Lauren, I remember being left in Milan by myself with sixteen trunks of runway samples to corral to the baggage check. I was essentially a pack mule with a wagon train of couture, carrying one-of-a-kind samples from an entire runway show. The anxiety I felt the entire flight from Italy, of potentially having suitcases of work items go missing, gave me a luggage-checking phobia I still have to this day. *"Stai bene?"* I remember the stewardess repeatedly asking me. All I could respond was "Yes, I'll have the rigatoni."

So when a friend of mine turned forty and a small group of us rented a sailboat to cruise the Mediterranean for a few days, I flew with a small carry-on of essentials (what more did I need than polka-dot swim trunks and Celine Dion's greatest hits, anyway?). My friends, however, showed up with a runway capsule collection for a two-week sojourn. Everyone brought gobs and gobs of luggage that had to be checked. All I could imagine was it sinking the boat.

Well, one of our crew lost his luggage (of course!), so every day, we'd sail to an island, then have to return to the Naples airport to inquire about his missing bags. It basically ruined our trip, which meant extra Campari. It was the kind of story Sophia would tell on a *Golden Girls* episode. The very last day, he got his bags back, but not until after he had an epiphany: As much as he loved his crazy wardrobe, he enjoyed the simplicity of rotating three borrowed outfits. As a consolation, everyone who worked at the Naples airport was hot and named Alessandro, which did make it all a little less painful.

Who's the man-eater now, *Jolene!* What else would I wear to see Ms. Parton but a Navajo leather jacket with fringe and conchos?

ARE WE THERE Yet?

No matter where you go, there's always something you should add to your suitcase . . . and subtract. I'm sure it's obvious which of these items may be flagged by security.

WHERE ARE YOU GOING?	Pack It	Leave It at Home	Best Accessory	Wild-Card Items
Disneyworld	Nike Air Max Siren Print sneaks, or Olivia slip-ons by MICHAEL Michael Kors (zappos.com)	White clothing. Three words: Raspberry. Lemonade. Slush.	Poncho, for Splash Mountain and Epcot's Drinking Around the World attraction	Tiara (you *are* at the Magic Kingdom!), Tums for churro abuse
Bahamas	Embellished, encrusted, envy-inducing sandals (dillards.com)	Silk tops or dresses. Silk *hateth* humidity.	Good luck jewelry for gambling at Atlantis	Eye-makeup remover, after gambling away little Johnny's college tuition
Europe	**London:** velvet blazer à la Kate Moss **Paris:** Ralph Lauren Slim-Fit Cotton Trench Coat **Rome:** moto jacket for being "abducted" by hot local on a Vespa	The American dollar (unless you're in Greece), backpack, flip-flops and Google Glass (you won't be allowed to shop at Harrods!)	Kate Spade passport holder (katespade.com)	One Direction concert T (for your, uh, niece), lingerie bag for Parisian purchases, empty duffel to fill with Prada outlet merch

WHERE ARE YOU GOING?	Pack It	Leave It at Home	Best Accessory	Wild-Card Items
Grand Canyon	Cute and comfy climbing gear by prAna (prana.com)	Anything with a slippery sole, contact lenses	GPS	Waterproof iPhone case, ski poles, canteen of white wine spritzer
The Alamo	MIA tall boots or ankle booties to wear with jeans and a tunic or sundress (nordstrom .com)	Short shorts and belly-baring tops, because no one wants to remember the "Ala-Ho"	Suede fringe hobo with zipper. Try Tarjay's affordable selection (target .com)	Kendra Scott Skylar earrings. She has a San Antonio outpost! (kendrascott.com)
Graceland	Ts and capris by day, lightweight dresses for river cruises and BBQs at night	Long-sleeve white jumpsuit— let's leave that unbreathable beast to The King.	Demeter Fragrance Library Banana Flambee perfume (demeterfragrance .com)	Push-up bra or corset plus fringe for heading east to Dollywood
Home for the holidays	Athleta Ponte Twill Moto Pant with a stretch waistband for stress eating (athleta.gap .com)	Splurges from the big city. Do you really need the scrutiny?	Downloaded TED talks about the art of diplomacy	Aleve, "personal massager"

CREATE YOUR OWN
cruise collection

At Ralph Lauren, we would design for spring, summer, fall, and "cruise," and I remember thinking, *Cruise? What's that?* It is just another name that designers use for their "resort" collections.

Originally created for women who would travel during the winter months to postcard-worthy places like Palm Beach and Bermuda, these high-end, between-season collections often have nautical or tropical-chic flavor. Think of a caftan-ed C. Z. Guest and Babe Paley sipping pineapple cocktails in Round Hill, Jamaica. Another round, Jeeves!

While cruise collections may be under the radar, cruise vacations are more popular than ever—in fact, I've been on over twenty, from Canada to Bermuda. Here are some fashionable tips so you don't think, *Oh, ship! What do I wear?*

ASK ABOUT DRESS CODES

On many cruises, there are at least two formal evenings—we're talking long gowns and tuxes. You can get away with wearing a little black dress, jewelry, and a pashmina for these events, but why not push the envelope? This is a boatload of people you may never see again in your life, so rock the sequins and plunging backs. Because of fire codes, no rooms have outlets for irons or steamers, so pack silk-knit jersey fabrics that are practically wrinkle-proof.

Style is something that each of us already has. All we need to do is find it.

DIANE VON FURSTENBERG

BRING THE RIGHT CASUAL WEAR

I literally have seen people spend a full week in their bathrobes—even at the buffet. That's not what I mean by casual chic. Tote along a resort-y bag for off-the-boat excursions, capris and a tunic, a cute athleisure outfit for your morning coffee and/or workout, and a sarong or caftan with your swimsuit. I love the ones from Calypso to take you to and from the pool like a pouty starlet on holiday (calypsostbarth.com). As legendary edit-rix Diana Vreeland said, caftans are "fashionable for the beautiful people." Without one, you might become one of the bathrobe people.

RUN WITH A THEME

Some cruises are designed around a theme, from dancing to culinary adventures. Find out if the cruise has a theme beforehand so you know to prepare or to run for the hills. I remember a woman named Linda who was possibly near seventy and a regular on *Dancing with the Stars* cruises. She showed up in full dancer regalia daily, ready for her close-up—and we all fell in love with her joie de vivre. While Linda's look was a little overboard, pardon the pun, embrace the theme of the cruise you choose. Say you're go-ing on one of those insanely popular Monsters of Rock cruises. Why not go all out with a studded jean jacket, shredded sleeveless concert T, dangly earrings, and faux-gold armband tattoo?

COMBAT WINDSWEPT HAIR

Ocean breezes are refreshing, but you could look like Hurricane Carson hit you without the right reinforcements. For formal evenings there are always salon services onboard, but for day I would invest in a fabulous hat (I love a wide-brimmed style like the one Amal Clooney was snapped in post Venetian wedding, or a straw fedora with a black band). They instantly add glamour and pack so well and recover their shape, especially the Floppy and the Squishee Classic (with built-in UPF) by hat genius Eric Javits (ericjavits.com).

SAVE YOUR STILETTOS

Not to go all *Titanic* on you, but I've literally had moments where I'm talking to someone in the hallway one minute, and we're nearly upside down the next. They call it "rough seas." I always sug-gest putting a thin layer of tread on the soles of your kitten heels *and* your embellished flats before your trip, so you don't skid down the football field length of the ship.

PACK FOR THE BIG CHILL

On my *Dancing with the Stars* cruise to Alaska, I was glad to have packed layers along with my bear repellent and pocket telescope to see Russia. Even if you go in summer, it's probably going to be a li'l nippy. Layering up is key for the Canadian Mari-times cruises as well. Pack a few cute sweaters and a navy or neutral-hued anorak that will look good thrown over anything. Land's End makes a really affordable one in a cute military style, in petite to plus sizes (landsend.com).

CHOOSE YOUR OWN WEDDING ADVENTURE:
what do I wear?

I get asked this question all the time, and the first thing I tell women is to think of a wedding like a movie set, where your outfit is part of the backdrop. The next thing I ask them is, "Who is the star?" (Answer: not you.) As a supporting cast member, you need to know what level of formality and friskiness is expected. Lights, camera, action!

WHO'S GETTING HITCHED?

A. Your girlfriend/roommate/crazy coworker, which means you can let your hair down. Trendy, glitzy, flirty—it's date night with the hubs or Bruno Marsing with people you love.

B. Colleague/boss/neighbor you have a formal relationship with, or your child/niece/relative, which means you want to look classic. They'll have these photos/impressions forever.

WHERE IS THE WEDDING?

1. Ceremony in a church or temple, with a black-tie reception following at a private club/hotel.

2. Indoor or outdoor ceremony, followed by a cocktail reception at a private club/hotel/home.

3. Island/destination with a cocktail reception at a hotel/beach following outdoor ceremony.

A + 1 = Foxy Formal
Since this is formal, slip into a long gown that is slinky, strapless, or backless (with cleavage cupcakes, of course). A halter looks classy from the front, sexy from the back. You can get away with a cocktail-length dress if it has beaded, lace, or crystal embellishments (try Marchesa Notte or ML Monique Lhuillier at saks.com). Spring and summer call for fluttery chiffon, lace, georgette, and crepe. Fall/winter means champagne, earth tones, black, and metallics. Look for silks (dupioni and shantung are textured enough to smooth over lumps), charmeuse, and satin in structured styles.

A + 2 = Sexy Cocktail
If you don't have a hot cocktail dress already hanging in your closet, this is your opportunity to invest in one that you'll wear again for New Year's, big-number birthdays, and on vacation. Your litmus tests should be "Do I feel sexy in this regardless of going up a few pounds?" and "Can I electric slide/hold champers and a bacon-wrapped date in this and feel totally comfortable?" Think about what's on-trend, from D&G bold florals to hot pink (which looks surprisingly good on many people) to formfitting styles with subtle cutouts.

A + 3 = Beach Bombshell

Choose brights, graphics, and reflective embellishments. A blinged-out caftan can work, or try a linen jumpsuit with a statement necklace with materials like bone, wood, and quartz by Lizzie Fortunato—so sleek and modern (lizziefortunato.com). Sexy strappy sandals plus an embellished flip-flop or wedge are musts so you don't sink into sand (I love Loeffler Randall's chic lace-up sandals and sexy wedges, loefflerrandall.com). Put your hair in sexy beach waves. If the bride and groom do ask guests to wear white, go for knee-length so your dress doesn't compete with the bride's, which I'm hoping is longer, not shorter.

- -

Tzuj Do It . . . Judith Leiber purses can be so Alexis Morrell Carrington Colby, which actually makes them beyond fab. As long as you're not wearing a bird/leopard/rock 'n' roll rubber duckie on your actual body, why not go wild with your accessories? Or in this case, Wild Kingdom (judithleiber.com).

- -

B + 1 = Flattering Formal

I still think a long dress is appropriate, but if you're petite and feel swallowed up by a long gown, cocktail-length can work if it has flair. Think: an A-line or bold neckline or bodice embellishment that gives an otherwise demure dress a dash of drama. Arm issues? Choose sheer illusion sleeves and three-quarter lace sleeves instead of a jacket, which adds bulk. Hose are banned unless it's a sheer black nylon with a pointy-toe stiletto in winter, though I'd still opt for a sandal peeking out from a long column or sheath dress. Whether you go long or short, David Meister is a reliable resource with a range of styles that work for virtually everyone (neimanmarcus.com).

B + 2 = Classic Cocktail

I'm all for navy, champagne, and metallic dresses any time of year. The trick is keeping your accessories season-specific and not matching them perfectly to your dress. No champagne dress and champagne shoes—go for a metallic or a nude. (Remember dyeables? I could die.) The only exception is the little black dress. In fall and winter, you can get away with black stilettos or strappy sandals with a hint of texture or sparkle. For spring and summer, lighten up your LBD with lighter neutrals and metallics.

B + 3 = Beach Chic

Think Lilly, Milly, Tory, and Trina, as far as frocks go. Woven matte silver or gold fabrics look good on every skin tone. If you love a maxi dress, here's your opportunity. If you're going with a darker hue like brown or navy, work in splashes of color through your wrap, bold earrings, a chunky beaded necklace (try wood beads for a fresh high-low mix), or colorful glasses. I love the idea of getting fancy specs just for special occasions and have seen many chic women do this. Forget black—it's a total drag on the sand.

- -

Tzuj Do It . . . Splurge on a vintage Hermès scarf; it'll kick up a little black dress and can even be knotted over a handbag like the French do. *Je suis!* You can find them on therealreal.com and also get lucky at your local consignment store.

- -

THIS IS so not APPROPRIATE (or is it?)

No matter where you're headed or what occasion your destination calls for, fashion etiquette has shifted from what you probably heard growing up. And if anyone's up for bucking the biggies, it's *moi*.

"You Can't Wear White Before Memorial Day/After Labor Day!"

Modern Reboot: If it's a basic like a pair of white jeans, you can ride 'em through September and wear them again in spring. And you know those creamy white wool pants and sweaters that Michael Kors does so well? Those can go all through the winter, too. It's only those full-on summer white bottoms and white dresses that you want to save for summer.

"You Must Wear All Black to a Funeral!"

Modern Reboot: It doesn't have to be black; it can be the darker hues of charcoal gray, navy, and dark brown. You want it to be quiet and respectful, so no large prints. But you don't need to look like the Sicilian grandma in the latest Dolce & Gabbana campaign.

"You Can't Have Long Hair After Forty!"

Modern Reboot: Gabrielle Union, Jennifer Garner, Julianne Moore, Kyle Richards, Penelope Cruz, and SJP would say *au contraire*. I'm not advocating following Crystal Gayle (who I happen to adore) down the Rapunzel path, but thick, healthy locks skimming your mid-back is always stylish. Forty *is* the new twenty-eight anyway. Just avoid scrunchies, headbands, and hair combs at all costs.

"No Open-Toe Shoes After Labor Day!"

Modern Reboot: According to Christian Louboutin and all the other great shoe gurus, your posh piggies may shine year-round. Wearing open-toe is a way of keeping things a little sexier but still demure enough to wear to work and appropriate in every season. Unless you're shoveling your driveway, the open-toe look can work in the winter if it's in a cool-weather material, like a suede strappy sandal with wool trousers.

"You Must Wear a Suit to a Job Interview!"

Modern Reboot: You want to look polished, but if you feel more "you" in a great blouse and cigarette pants than a typical suit, follow your instincts. In the media and creative worlds, a suit might even look too uptight. If you feel pressured to don one, don't go totally androgynous. Add a leopard-print heel or a snakeskin belt to give your suit a little swagger.

"You Can't Wear White or Ivory to a Wedding!"

Modern Reboot: While it's never a good idea to wear solid white or ivory, you can certainly get away with wearing a dress that has a white or ivory background if the non-white print is the dominant factor. Some color-block designs rely on panels of white to neutralize a harsh black or candy-bright dress, and that's totally kosher.

WHY *buy* WHEN YOU CAN *rent?*

In real estate bubbles and wear-it-once-or-twice fashion moments like weddings, graduations, and charity galas, it often doesn't pay to buy outright. That's why luxury rental sites are one of the biggest secrets of stylish women worldwide. They're the ideal destination for demo-ing a bag, dress, or accessory. No doorman or utilities included.

bagborroworsteal.com

This is the candy store of clutches, satchels, messengers, and more. Let's say you want a bag with more bling. Rent a Michael Kors bag with gold lock and chain accents to see how you feel. Or if you know a Fendi Baguette would be the perfect addition to an outfit you have planned for a big event, don't buy . . . rent it for a month and tote it to three more girls' dinners. Rental items aren't eligible for purchase, but you can snag items on the site, from "pristine" to "pre-loved," and sales can go up to over 70 percent off!

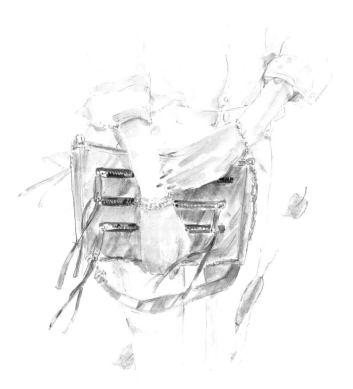

renttherunway.com

It's a perfect equation: low cash outlay for a you're-so-money look. They've also introduced a $139/month unlimited subscription that entitles you to receive up to three items from your style queue. Keep it for a week or half a year—and *they* dry-clean it afterward. My fave feature of the site is the customer photos you'll find with each look, where people give the skinny on how an item fits and feels. This is ideal when you're trying a new designer and are in need of real feedback.

gwynniebee.com

Curvy gals in the know rely on this rental site for on-trend plus-size clothing (from 10 to 32) because of its quality brands and easy-to-use format. Start a subscription (there are choices), build a "closet," and for a flat fee, you'll get unlimited free shipping and exchanges (they include an envelope with postage, PTL!). If you fall in love with an item, you can purchase it at a discount. What's so helpful is how they arrange clothing by category, based on your shape or the specific occasion. And there's a thirty-day free trial. What's not to love?

carson confession: REESE'S PIECES

Why do celebrities borrow dresses from designers for major events? They get a guaranteed unique look, they save a bundle (yes, celebs do like to save!), and they avoid getting called out in mags for wearing the same gown twice (a serious sin in Hollywood). My cute-as-a-Tory Burch-button girlfriend from the East Coast was invited to attend the 2015 Oscars and wanted to look red-carpet amazing. But she didn't want to drop thousands on a dress she knew she would only wear once. She decided to try Rent the Runway and said she was blown away by how easy the whole process was. For $250 they shipped the dress in two sizes (just in case), along with knockout earrings and a clutch. She had it all sent to Los Angeles so she wouldn't have to lug it on the plane, and since she was petite, she used the hemming tape they provided in case the dress was too long (which it was). Her major "love my dress" moment happened when her Facebook page started blowing up as friends uploaded live television screenshots of her on the red carpet, standing behind none other than Reese Witherspoon . . . who was in a nearly identical white-and-black dress by Tom Ford. Legally blonde and legally brilliant!

BUTT seriously . . .

There are many events where "sitting pretty" is the name of the game, since you're spending most of the event on your arse. Think: graduations, christenings, baby showers. The key is wearing fabrics that don't give you "swamp butt" in warmer months, pardon my French Creole. Steer clear of silk, rayon, and nylon, especially in light colors that can't camouflage sweat marks, and stick to natural fibers like cotton and linen.

DATE NiGHT Dos

Whether it's "Netflix and chill," a concert, or samba lessons, the night will go twice as nice when you wear things that make you feel movie-premiere pretty.

Do: Put on killer heels—they'll lengthen your whole silhouette, which is always attractive. No time for a pedi? A pointy stiletto goes a long way.

Do: Try a top that opens up your chest and shoulder area and draws attention to your collarbone, which I'm sure you dusted with a little bronzing powder. Cleavage is optional, only if you feel "you" when your tatas are on display.

Do: Put on metallic fabrics, tops with embellishments, or light-catching jewelry (but not all three). At night, you're going to reflect whatever light sources are bouncing off of those items, which gives your face more sparkle.

Do: Wear pants, skirts, and dresses that mold to your shape, not drape over your body. It's dark— only your silhouette will matter, not whether the backs of your legs are bulging in leather leggings.

Do: Dress differently than you would for a day date (i.e., no wedges, flats, cardis, or maxi dresses). Nighttime is for slinkier fabrics. Jeans work if you stick to dark washes and pair them with a great boot or heel.

Do: Play up your features with highlighter, lip-liner and gloss, and smoky eyes. You'll learn all about how to apply them from the beauty gurus in chapter 7.

Tszuj Do It... Dream in date wear! Instead of counting sheep, count the number of nighttime outfits you can create from your existing wardrobe and accessories. It'll either put you right to sleep or take the pressure off when Gerard Butler comes to pick you up in his Mercedes. Hey, I can dream, too.

happy-hour time:
WHAT MATCHES MY MARGARITA?

When you can't dash home after work before the clock strikes 5:00 P.M. and glasses start getting rimmed with salt, it's time to improvise. The secret to transitioning from desk to drinks is knowing what to switch out for maximum impact.

Shoes: Give suit pants or a pencil skirt some edge by swapping boots or kitten heels for stilettos (think: animal print, tiny gold grommets, or cobalt suede). Plan your pants or skirt for the day with your P.M. shoe choice in mind.

Jewelry: Put on sparkly earrings with pretty stones. Throw on a collar necklace that will dress up a button-down. Ditch your everyday watch and layer up with bangles. I love chunky clip-ons by Jennifer Miller (jennifermillerjewelry.com) and bracelets by Alexis Bittar (alexisbittar.com).

Bag: Stash your boxy work bag in the office and transfer just your phone, wallet, keys, and makeup to an oversize clutch. Snakeskin and taupe are neutrals that work year-round with everything from jeans to all black.

Top: Swap your blouse for a slinky tank or dressed-up T that will liven up your work blazer. Or do my favorite faux-suit trick: Wear a black crepe wrap-top jumpsuit with a fitted jacket for work and whip off the jacket for nighttime.

Pants: Sometimes all it takes is switching from suit pants to jeans. Everything can stay the same—even a plain button-down. Just roll the sleeves, pop the collar, and throw on a fabulous necklace or boho-chic scarf.

- -

BUTT seriously . . .

Make your four-plus-inch stilettos more foot-friendly by taking a quarter inch off of the heel. Trained cobblers can do this without compromising the structure of the shoe. That little quarter inch makes all the difference. Or so they tell me.

- -

RANDOM ACTS OF
Stylishness

Sometimes you can't help finding yourself in unusual circumstances. Like the time I dressed for an L.A. Clippers game looking half Braveheart, half tomato soup can (Google it). When in Rome . . .

RANDOM SITUATION	What to Wear
Court appearances/ arraignments	Don a discreet evil-eye necklace or bracelet to ward off negativity. Tailored Theory suit with a good blow-out and patent pumps. Although big hair and a grommet sweater totally worked for Marisa Tomei in *My Cousin Vinny*. Just sayin'.
Driver's-license photo	Simple collared shirt from J.Crew or Theory (think Anne Hathaway, not Anne Boleyn). Pop the collar to frame your face. No stripes, which scream "jail me" if you get pulled over. BTW, are you still getting carded? Totes jeals.
World's largest yard sale	Dress down to get a better deal. Hat, sunglasses, slip-on sneaks, skip the money belt. Novelty T that's a convo starter with chatty sellers. Cute cargo pants with lots of pockets for tchotchkes.
Shooting a free-throw at an Indiana Pacers game	A Tory Burch tunic (toryburch.com) or Vince. cardigan with leggings is camera-friendly and athletic. No crop tops for obvious reasons. A cushioned wedge bootie will give you "air," Jordan.
Guest appearance on *Wheel of Fortune*	No dangling sleeves or bangle bracelets that can get caught in the wheel. How about a kelly-green wrap dress that screams "Show me the money!"
Meeting with your ex and divorce attorneys	Heels, skirt, and low-cut top that can be used as a distraction tactic when you're in the hot seat for _____ (fill in the blank). Skip the jewelry—you want alimony. Good manicure for finger pointing.
Renaissance Faire	*Game of Thrones* chic: an Alanis Morrisette middle part, gold bangles, velvet blazer in merlot that will camouflage mutton juice and mead. Good morrow!
Nudist retreat	Duh.

WHAT TO WEAR TO YOUR *high school reunion*

Heightened expectations, old flames, and mean girls—this is major. Make up for lost time with some serious style strategy.

Tenth: Dress to impress. You want to show everyone you've "made it." Cashmere, leather, great designer bag, great heels are on the menu. Make your high school ex sorry he dumped you like day-old pizza by deploying the ultimate outfit accessory: a shirtless pic of your current love as your iPhone screensaver. Don't have a guy who looks good shirtless? Download a half-naked faux beau. Name him Hans.

Twentieth: By your twentieth, if you have to dress like you've made it, you haven't. Think casual chic. Gravity (and pregnancies) have started to pull things down, so the key is contouring pieces that lift and support. Mom jeans are not an option. Wrap dresses, slinky Theory tops, and skinny jeans with stiletto boots are in. Speaking of which, did you see that the prom queen looks like State Fair Barbie and the star quarterback is bald 'n' bloated? Schadenfreude for all!

Fiftieth: Just show up. You're still alive! Yay you! For bonus points, dress like you're going back to your twentieth reunion, but with the sexual fire of your tenth. After all, these are the Viagra years—who knows what could happen! Start with a gravity-defying outfit. I like an embellished knit top with a tailored jacket and great jewelry. Don't forget heels. Everyone else shrank two inches, but you don't have to.

Tszuj Do It... Enjoy some "merchantainment." Step into stores that are creative and fun and transport you to another world just by the way they're styled. You can be Lady Mary Crawley from *Downton Abbey* in the Anglo-Waspy world of Ralph Lauren, a sexy Bond girl from Agent Provocateur, or a boho hipster from Anthropologie. Even if that world is so not you, it's almost like being cast in a play, where you can take on that persona for ten minutes. You never know when you might need to get into character.

COSTUME-PARTY *Pointers*

We all know what a buzzkill it is when people don't dress up for a costume party. Wait, are *you* that buzzkill? Must fix that right now.

ARABIAN NIGHTS

This is the one and only time I'll suggest wearing harem pants. The key is finding a flattering, inexpensive street version that looks more Princess Jasmine than MC Hammer. Or check out H&M, Forever 21, and Etsy for harem styles that you'll be comfortable pairing with a T and strappy sandals (hm.com; forever21.com; etsy.com). If you're bottom-heavy, put the party on the top with a patterned metallic top and your business on the bottom with a full black Gypsy skirt.

SEVENTIES DISCO

Mine your local consignment store for Pucci and psychedelic prints—even a groovy headscarf and hoop earrings will do the trick. You could take a DVF wrap you already own and add wedges, bold gold jewelry, oversize round glasses, and an Afro wig—you'll look totally seventies glam. Or consider a BCBG caftan (bcbg.com). If you buy something that is borderline seventies but still totally "now," you'll wind up wearing it more than once.

TOTALLY EIGHTIES

There are so many easy ways to do eighties. I'd think of the three main theme options: touches of neon (think: a pump, jellies, rubber bracelets, sunglasses), Madonna circa *Like a Virgin* (lace headband, black bra, pearls, off-the-shoulder top), and punk rock (mousse, wayfarer glasses, rocker T). So much of this stuff is in thrift and vintage stores right now, so go all out. Channel your favorite

eighties star, from Molly Ringwald in a gunnysack prom dress to Debbie Harry in punk perfection.

BAD CHRISTMAS-SWEATER PARTY

The key is keeping the sweater tight. No matter how ugly the pattern is, if it hugs you in the right places, like your bust and waistline, you're going to look kitschy hot. Pair it with skinny jeans, cute boots, and a voluminous blowout and you might actually pull off Valerie Bertinelli in *One Day at a Time*. When you're hunting, look in the teen or children's section for a tighter fit. Just make sure you won't be popping out all night, which can ruin and/or make a party.

HAWAIIAN LUAU

Relax—you don't have to wear a grass skirt and a coconut bra or a hideous Hawaiian shirt to look legit (they're best left to Magnum P.I.). You can find really inexpensive maxi dresses with big florals on HSN and QVC (hsn.com; qvc.com). They look really pretty, and you can actually wear them again with a jean jacket and wedges. Bonus points: Go to your florist and get a real lei made with a hearty flower like an orchid or white carnation, then have a giant one tucked into your hair. *Mahalo!*

KENTUCKY DERBY

While the Kentucky Derby is a day steeped in tradition, thoroughbreds, and mint juleps it's also, quite simply, a Mad Hatter costume party! Nyquist may be the most recent winner of the Derby, but with a head-turning ensemble, you're next in line. Look at this as a chance to let your freak flag fly . . . in pastels. How do you look chic without turning your head into an Easter basket? Follow these tips: Choose a hat that suits your face shape, pick a strong color that you can repeat in subtle notes throughout your outfit to tie it all together, and make sure the fit is comfortable enough that you won't fidget while wearing it.

Speaking of feeling more comfortable in your skin, how can you rock all the fierce, fabulous, and wacky looks we've just discussed if you don't feel great about what's happening underneath? In the next chapter, you're going to hear from some amazing experts, from the one and only "Bra Whisperer" to a professional plus-size model, to one of my favorite people on earth—who happens to be a former showgirl—all in the name of body confidence. Don't you think it's about time we got naked? We've shared five beautiful chapters together, and I think we're ready.

With *O* magazine's Gayle King and Robert Herjavec of *Shark Tank* at the 2016 Kentucky Derby.

carson confession: COSTUME BALLS

For those who don't know, Fire Island is like a gay fairy island where people go in the summer and still throw elaborate costume parties. We'd make hand-made costumes with spray-painted shoes and pants from metallic camouflage. By the end of the evening our costumes were always destroyed. I don't remember that much, but I know we always had a fabulous time. There was always a theme, from *Spartacus* to *The Wizard of Oz* (naturally) to outer space. Yes, we actually dressed up as visitors from . . . wait for it . . . Uranus! The little head-bands with penises on them that you'd wear to a bachelorette party? Of course we had those. Then there was the time I dressed like Mr. Peanut, complete with cane and top hat. I was totally into that, by the way. The bottom line is have fun with your alter ego. A costume gives you the chance to be someone totally different for the night. If you're shy, the key is incorporating street clothing into your costume so you still feel comfortable while giving a nod to the theme.

OMGG: Oh My Greek God! At this Fire Island fete, my friends and I celebrated toga-therness.

6.
Oh, MY BOD!
ROCK Those Curves

*I feel very comfortable in my own skin.
When someone makes jokes about
me being heavy, it makes me mad.
It's not true. I'm right where I should be.*

AMY SCHUMER

- -

FULL DISCLOSURE: I HAVE NOT BEEN around a lot of naked women in my lifetime. So when I was asked to host the show *How to Look Good Naked* for Lifetime television, I asked myself if I was really up to the challenge. Of course I knew the secret to looking good naked: "A box of wine and a dimmer switch!" I told the producers, but I was secretly shaking in my Emporio Armani tighty-whities, wondering if I'd have to give anyone a Brazilian.

Thank God I went through with it, though, because I got a boatload of behind-the-scenes body-image intel from women of every size, color, age, and background. The common theme? Body shaming. Lots of it. You lug your baggage with

you everywhere you go. It comes with you to the store when you shop (*Ugh! This looks awful on me*), to the gym when you work out (*Will I ever lose these flabby, bat-wing arms?*), to restaurants with friends (*Oh, just a salad please, balsamic vinegar on the side; leave the croutons and I'll kill you*), and to the bedroom (*Turn around / Turn off the lights / Yes, dammit, the nightlight, too*).

This kind of negative lingo has become the new normal. American women are so bombarded with images of perfection, from television to billboards to airbrushed celeb Instagrams, that it's not hard to see why.

When I worked with Layla, an adorable, vivacious twenty-something on the pilot episode of *How to*

On *How to Look Good Naked* with a bevy of soon-to-be body-confident women.
My white underwire bra was at the cleaners.

Look Good Naked, her body confidence was at level 0. Layla was just starting out in the workforce in Southern California and more than ever needed her body confidence to catch up with the kind of confidence her bosses would demand of her every day on the job. Growing up, she unfortunately had a very domineering and competitive mother who always nitpicked her about what she ate, saying things like, "Oh, are you going to eat some more? You should probably dial it back; you're starting to get a little heavy." Her mom had no clue that she planted a seed that would bloom into Layla's full-blown body dysmorphia. By the time we began filming the show, she could barely stand to look at her body, much less without clothes.

Okay, this is the part where I start to sound like a royal jerk. But stay with me here. We put Layla in a room with three-way mirrors and asked her to disrobe down to her bra and panties. From head to toe, we invited her to critique her own body. She started going like a freight train that wouldn't stop: "My cheeks are too full; my bust is okay but I could probably use a reduction; I have this big scar on my stomach; my butt is too big; my thighs are too dimpled. . . ." It was one big pity party.

Layla was so down on her body, she couldn't see things accurately anymore. And she's not alone. According to research, up to eight out of ten women are dissatisfied with their reflection, and more than half may see a distorted image. More often than not, women would wind up crying to me in this freaky funhouse with bad flourescent lighting, and I would ask myself, *What am I doing to these women?*

But then, like clockwork, the breakthrough would happen. It always wound up being the pivotal and most transformational point of the show. That's when we would take a really honest look at her body in those mirrors and together, say, "Yes, there are definitely some flaws, but nobody's perfect. Not even those fifteen-year-old Latvian models you think are perfect." (Trust me, I've seen those Latvian models, and even *they* don't look like their airbrushed selves in magazines). It was all about getting the negatives out in the open so she could move to the positives. Eventually, she could agree with me that she had a beautiful smile, strong legs, and smooth, healthy skin.

To keep the momentum, we jumped into Layla's makeover process. Initially, she would say, "No, I can't wear that," and "No, that color doesn't look good on me," and "No, I don't wear patterns." She was so full of roadblocks because she'd convinced herself that nothing was going to look good on her. But after pushing past her own barricades and being more open to trying things on, she would look again at her reflection and say, "Huh. Maybe I don't look so bad in this." At our final try-on, the "I don't look so bad" turned into "Well, I look pretty good!" and by the end of the show, she was ready for her real test: a nude photo shoot. For a billboard. In Times Square. I am not kidding. Just be glad it wasn't me.

Layla wasn't exactly jumping for joy at the thought of a magnified version of her naked body plastered on the side of a building. But we helped her look amazing with lighting, makeup, hair-stylists, photographers, and took the most gorgeous photos, one of which made it onto the billboard. Layla almost fainted when she saw

it. I egged her on to ask strangers, "What do you think of me up there?" People would make comments like, "Wow, you have a nice rack" (guys just say the sweetest things!), "Great legs," or "That is a fierce pose." She got so much positive feedback from friends, family, and perfect strangers that together we were able to reprogram her to tune out the negative voices in her head.

One of my goals of this chapter is to help you face your body baggage head-on and kick it to the curb like Layla did. The key is making an effort to be nicer to your body, to accept what you love and what you want to work on—and own that. Just because you may not be thrilled with the size of your boobs, your thighs, or your tummy doesn't mean you should give up, pop a pint of Ben & Jerry's, throw on a Snuggie, and say "Whatever." You have every right to enjoy fashion and to feel sexy, fabulous, and comfortable, whether you're a size 2 or 22.

Speaking of sizes, there's been a lot of chatter about the term "plus size." Do we even need it? I mean, sizes 0, 2, and 4 aren't called "minus size." Instead of obsessing about numbers, why not shift the focus to feeling strong and healthy? Some people are healthy at a size 0 and others are at a size 18.

Being skinny doesn't mean that you're more healthy, and being heavier doesn't mean that you're not. Having a positive attitude toward yourself, self-helpy as it sounds, reflects much more about you than the number on a scale. People don't think, *Wow, Penelope looks like she's 149 pounds today.* But they will think you look great if you're radiant and confident and wearing your favorite color. Or, they'll be secretly jealous because you look so—*gasp*—happy. That's the power of dressing well and feeling it and radiating that good energy out to the world. Or even just to the sweet toothless man at your corner deli.

WHAT'S YOUR
nude attitude?

Answer true or false for each of these questions:

☐ **1.** I won't wear a bathing suit/bikini in front of most of my friends.

☐ **2.** I have a worse day if the scale tells me I'm up two pounds.

☐ **3.** I loathe stripping down in dressing rooms and rarely go anymore.

☐ **4.** I have a running list in my head of all my body flaws.

☐ **5.** I critique my own reflection when I catch myself after a shower.

☐ **6.** I pay more attention to covering parts of my body during sex than how it feels.

☐ **7.** I rarely show my upper arms or legs above the knee.

☐ **8.** I tell people they're crazy when they say I look good or ask if I've lost weight.

☐ **9.** I don't really like photographs taken of me . . . especially ones in summer.

☐ **10.** I buy bras and underwear for utility only, not to look or feel sexy.

If you had more than one true, you need a new nude attitude. Let us begin!

Back when I was modeling, the first time I went to Italy, I was having cappuccinos every day, and I gained fifteen pounds. And I felt gorgeous! I would take my clothes off in front of the mirror and be like, "Oh, I look like a woman," and I felt beautiful, and I never tried to lose it, because I loved it.

CHRISTINA HENDRICKS

ANANSA SIMS'S *Five body commandments*

Anansa Sims is the daughter of legendary supermodel Beverly Johnson, the first African American model to grace the cover of *Vogue*. Anansa, an inspiring and successful plus-size model who openly shares her struggles with body image, in hopes of strengthening young girls' self-esteem, has just as much to feel proud about as her mom. Commit to following Anansa's body commandments, starting today.

Anansa's fierce message: Get comfortable with your body, no matter what the scale says.

COMMANDMENT 1:
Thou Shalt Shop for the Body You Have Now

"So many people think, *When I lose this ten pounds, I'm going to do or wear x, y, and z.* You're putting your life on hold for this moment that may never come. The crazy thing is if you do get to that moment, then you're ready for the next ten pounds, and you're never satisfied. Go out and get the cute clothes in the size you are now, not the size you wish you were. With everything that I preach and I know, I actually just did that to myself. I bought a pair of jeans in a size smaller than usual, thinking I'd been working out and eating right and that would only continue. Then I wore them out on a date with my husband, and I could barely breathe in them. I'm sitting in the movies, I've got them unbuttoned, and already I'm feeling bad about myself. All I could think was, *I like the way I look but I don't like the way I feel.* So I bought the same jeans one size bigger the next day. Who cares that they were bigger? It was ridiculous. I had to check myself."

COMMANDMENT 2:
Thou Shalt Not Judge Thyself by a Number

"I was unpacking boxes of my old clothes before I had my children, and I would say 75 percent of my clothes had the inside tags cut off. I forgot that I used to do that. I hated looking at a bigger number than a size 8. Mentally I was always trained, with my mom being a model and my being exposed to the entertainment industry, that double digits are something to hide. I was always worried I'd leave them lying around and my boyfriend or my friends would see what size I really was. Opening those boxes was a trip. It made me think about all the extremes we go to because we judge ourselves. A friend moaned to me that she gained weight and I asked, 'Well, did you get on a scale?' She said, 'Oh, no, I don't want to be depressed.' Why does any number have to be depressing? I know it's easier said than done, but pick yourself up instead. I always feel better when I get my nails done or put on a cute outfit, which I do less these days as a mother of three, and forget how good it feels. When I catch myself in the mirror I think, *Oh, yeah, I'm pretty cute*. It's amazing what a little effort can do."

COMMANDMENT 3:
Thou Shalt Not Food-Shame Thyself

"I spent six months struggling to make it as a 'straight model,' which means non-plus size, by starving myself. I would eat half an apple a day or a bowl of soup, and people would tell me how great I looked, but I had never felt worse in my life. I wasn't healthy. When I let my body be the weight it naturally wanted to be, I started getting more jobs than ever as a plus-size model, which gave me back my confidence. I don't battle myself like I used to. I don't punish myself for eating the chocolate M&M's out of a pack of trail mix. If I feel like I've gone overboard after going to restaurants or just haven't been eating well, I drink a lot of water, I eat cleaner, and I exercise the next day. Or I take a walk with my husband, old-school style. I don't make it drama and a reason to hate on myself. Focus on what you can do tomorrow to get back on track."

COMMANDMENT 4:
Thou Shalt Get a Body Mantra

"I've always been comfortable walking around the house naked. I grew up in a 'naked' family and always had confidence. But all of that shifted when I went on my first lingerie shoot as a plus-size model. I thought to myself, *This isn't like my favorite lingerie at home. The cut of this underwear and full-coverage bra is not sexy or flattering.* I froze getting up there with all the cameras and people around me. But then I reminded myself over and over again during the shoot, *They hired me because they want* me. Then the shoot started getting fun, and hearing people say, "Gorgeous, Anansa!" felt like something I could actually hear and believe. I remember my mom used to stick little affirmations on the mirror when I was growing up, so I'd feel strong and confident. Whatever props you can give yourself over and over, whatever will stick in your mind and stay there will slowly change it. Say something positive enough times and you will eventually believe it."

COMMANDMENT 5:
Thou Shalt Ignore the Haters

"I remember doing a *Glamour* photo shoot with other curvy models, and we got such positive feedback. But there was this minority of people who would rip us apart online, saying 'Do you think it's positive to show overweight women to young girls, and tell them it's okay to be fat?' Those comments hurt. And it's not just from strangers. I remember having a boyfriend in my twenties whose mother told him that if we got married, the curvy body I had then that seemed cute would become a disaster after I got older and had kids. He actually listened to her! I remember thinking both of them were crazy. I'm glad he didn't end up as my husband. The man I married loves me for who I am and thinks I look just as good in sweats and no makeup with a bun on my head as I do dolled up in high heels. Surround yourself with people who lift you up."

COMING UP
the Curve

It's high time more designers made fabulous clothing for women that isn't size prohibitive. I know most of these brands sound like a new and exciting prescription drug designed to prevent restless leg syndrome, but they're ultrafashionable resources for women with curves.

CARMAKOMA

If you like chic, tailored, and understated with just a touch of edge, carmakoma.com is a don't-miss destination. I think of it as a Theory or Vince for sizes through 24. The site is simple, luxurious, and well edited, so you won't get overwhelmed by options. The 70-percent-off sales and free shipping over $100 aren't bad, either!

ELOQUII

Eloquii.com has deeply discounted designer looks in sizes 14 to 24, along with a size 26 and 28 lookbook. What I love most about this site is its attitude: It reinforces that women of all sizes should have fun with their wardrobe, from body-con dresses to bold prints.

KIYONNA

Kiyonna.com's day and night dress selections and separates are strong. There's no way you won't find a flattering ruched or wrap top here. I recommend browsing their Most Loved section to see what other people have been buying. On a mission for next year's vacay wardrobe? They have a Black Friday sale in the middle of summer. Scoop up figure-flattering suits and caftans.

> Women come in all sizes. Seventy percent of women in the United States are a size 14 or above, and that's technically "plus size," so you're taking your biggest category of people and telling them, 'You're not really worthy."
>
> **MELISSA McCARTHY**

SEVEN7 BY MELISSA McCARTHY

The comedic rock star also has a talent for fashion design, and a positive message to boot: Don't marginalize the majority of American women! Melissa's namesake brand has sizes 4 through 28 and is carried at hsn.com, lanebryant.com, macys.com, and nordstrom.com.

HOT SHAPEWEAR *Tips* FROM *Heather Thomson*

Yes, the first step in body love is being happy with yourself. But loving yourself doesn't mean you can't take steps to feel more confident in your clothing. No matter what your size, having the right foundation is key. I asked my buddy, *Real Housewives of New York* alum Heather Thomson, about the latest in shapewear, as well as her top picks from her ultraversatile line, Yummie by Heather Thomson (yummielife.com).

CK: What's the biggest myth about shapewear?

HT: Smaller is better. Sizing down can actually cause you to have more trouble than you started with and is definitely not comfortable. You shouldn't be using shapewear to change who you are but to be the best you that you can be. As much as looking good is feeling good, feeling good is mandatory to looking good. So think *wow* not *ow*, and buy true to size!

CK: Can shapewear, you know, come out of the closet?

HT: Yes! The idea of having to hide your shapewear seemed antiquated to me. I design pieces that are meant to be seen, are attitude-boosting, and are easy to incorporate while adding an element of style. It starts with the right foundation, like your bra and panties, slip, or hosiery, plus everyday essentials like my patented three-panel tank or 360-degree shaping Milan Legging that eliminates the need for a second layer. I also created jeans, activewear, and loungewear so you look great morning, noon, and night. Fashion doesn't have to hurt, and it doesn't have to come at a price. You can look good and feel good at the same time—that's a winning combination.

Holla! Heather knows it's what's inside that counts . . . which is why she developed a "core-drobe" for women.

CK: What Yummie products do you swear by?

HT: I don't ever wear a dress without a Yummie slip under it, and I start each day with a Yummie bra and panties. The products I design are truly for feel-good confidence to wear out, underneath, or alone.

bust booster

tummy slimmer

thigh shaper

CK: I'm going to name problem areas women often complain to me about, and you tell me the shapewear solution. . . .

PROBLEM: Saggy tush
HT: I like products that offer zoned compression, that lift and help to highlight your best areas. Also, pocket placements that give optical illusions of a lifted rear work wonders.
Heather's picks: Audra Mid-Waist Short, Yummie Denim Jeans

PROBLEM: Lumpy thighs
HT: Any type of smoother, like a slip or thigh shaper under a dress or skirt, will help to give the body a sleek, polished finish with every look.

Heather's picks: Yulia High Waist Skirt Slip, Margie Mid-Waist Thigh Shaper

PROBLEM: Lower tummy pooch
HT: I think the best way to control this trouble spot is to start with a shaping tank that offers firm control around the middle, paired with a shaping short. I like to call this Double Yummie!
Heather's picks: Original Yummie Tummie patented three-panel tank, Audra Mid-Waist Short

PROBLEM: Back fat
HT: Start with a great-fitting bra, so you don't create more of a problem. Then look for flattering everyday essentials like tanks and camis that will slim and shape where you need it.
Heather's picks: Yummie bras, Stephanie 2-Way Tank

Tszuj Do It... Have tasteful, professional photos taken of yourself semiclothed . . . or in the buff. See how much lighting, makeup, and strategic poses do for you, just like they do for top models. You don't have to show the final pics to anyone if you don't want to, but they'll look so good, you probably will.

carson confession:
MY FULL MONTY

Back when we were filming *Queer Eye*, I was told by our producers that our next makeover subject was a nudist. When he answered the door naked, I fought every urge to say, "Hello, Long Duck Dong." To really understand someone's psychology, I've always said that you have to first walk in their shoes (or in this case, no shoes . . . not even a cute merkin). So after some prayer and a little Kahlúa in my latte, I stripped down, too (thank goodness the cameras blurred out my man parts for television). When my colleagues Kyan, Jai, Ted, and Thom saw me in Garden of Eden mode, they freaked and locked me out of the house. So there I was, standing outside in suburban New Jersey, butt naked. After the initial self-consciousness wore off, it actually felt kind of freeing. And airy.

BUTT *seriously* . . .

Mark Twain may not have been talking about muffin tops when he said, "Comparison is the death of joy," but it totally applies if you're measuring yourself against Gisele or Rihanna! Don't hold yourself up to an unrealistic standard. Celebs don't even look like that, so why would you think you could or should? Work on being the best version of you.

When things get dark, when you feel really crappy about yourself or your body or how you look, sometimes a good way to get out of it is to have some gratitude. What I mean by that is, if you could go around your body and thank it for what it gives you, and thank yourself for your great eyesight or your thick hair or your nice legs, or your strong teeth, or whatever it is that you have that you were given, and make friends with those parts of your body and not try to focus on the parts that will never change.

AMY POEHLER

Wearing the right bra is crucial to having a sleek silhouette. Susan Nethero, aka the "Bra Whisperer," shares an eye-opening fact: Over 85 percent of women are wearing the wrong-size bra! Follow this chart to see if you're properly harnessing your tatas.

ARE YOU BRA SAVVY?

start
HAVE YOU EVER BEEN PROFESSIONALLY FITTED FOR A BRA?

SOMETIMES WHEN I'M RUNNING

DO YOUR STRAPS EVER FALL DOWN?

NOT UNLESS I WANT THEM TO!

DO YOU EVER TOSS YOUR BRAS IN THE DRYER?

NO

YES

HOW LONG AGO?

LESS THAN A YEAR

MORE THAN A YEAR

WHAT TYPES OF BRAS DO YOU OWN?

WHAT ABOUT WASHING THEM?

IN YOUR EVERYDAY BRAS, DO YOUR BOOBS SAG OR HANG LOWER THAN THE MIDPOINT BETWEEN YOUR SHOULDERS AND ELBOW?

NO

YES

HAVE YOU HAD KIDS, HORMONE CHANGES, OR WEIGHT LOSS/GAIN SINCE THEN?

NO

THE ONE BASIC STYLE THAT SUITS ME BEST, PLUS A PUSH-UP

WASH BY HAND IN COLD WITH LINGERIE WASH

YES

MACHINE WASH IN COLD

TRUE OR FALSE: MY BACK STRAP RIDES UP WHEN MY BRA IS TOO BIG FOR ME.

TRUE

ROOM TO FIT ANY DOUGH IN THE TOP OF YOUR BRA CUP?

T-SHIRT, PUSH-UP, SHEER, CONVERTIBLE, CONTOURED CUPS

DO YOU REGULARLY WEAR THE SAME BRA TWO DAYS IN A ROW?

FALSE

HOW MANY BRAS DO YOU HAVE ON ROTATION?

DO YOU USE A MESH BAG?

MY AMEX, VISA, AND MC

JUST A BENJAMIN, BABY

WHERE SHOULD THE MAJORITY OF SUPPORT COME FROM IN YOUR BRA?

YEP, MY GIRLS SEEM TO BE HOLDING IT TOGETHER.

−5

+5

YES

NO

STRAPS

BACK BAND

NO, MY BRAS NEED REST, LIKE ME.

THE BOTTOM SUPPORT BAND WIDTH

JUMPING FROM A 34C TO A 36C, WHAT BRA PART GETS BIGGER?

SORRY, BRA

THE BOTTOM SUPPORT BAND AND ONE INCH OF DEPTH IN CUP

BRA-VO!

TRAINING BRA

When it comes to bra basics, what can we say? You're busted. You may think it doesn't make a difference if you buy a size off or toss your undergarments in the dryer, but they just won't hold up—or help you look or feel younger, shapelier, and slimmer, all in one. Go for a complimentary sizing at your local lingerie boutique or department store, pronto.

You realize a bra is more than a fabric sling to stick your girls, but there's still room to upgrade. You may not have taken the time to get resized lately, so see if there's any tweaking to be done. Put a little more attention into picking specialized styles—like a convertible bra for a racer-back tank or a corset style that will have you curving in and out in a strapless dress.

You have all the intel it takes to make sure your assets are well supported, from getting sized to using a fab lingerie wash (I love thelaundress.com). Now it's time to spice it up. There are so many brands competing for your attention, why not experiment with a color or cut that is edgier than your usual style? It may wind up being your new favorite thing in your drawer.

BREAST FRIENDS *Forever!*

These "bra-cessories" are the perfect pairings to keep on rotation with all your great-fitting new bras.

BREAST PETALS

Buy a pair of breast petals to keep your headlights from causing a traffic jam. If you have a thin bra or are wearing no bra at all, these little stick-on florettes do the trick. But don't just slap them on; you have to take the soft middle part and push in the nipple and then smooth the petal down (target.com or kohls.com).

LE LUSION ADHESIVE PLUNGE CUPS

Hello, J.Lo! When you want to wear a plunging neckline without a back strap or pesky fastener in between your tatas, these soft foam cups with silicone adhesive keep your plums, peaches, or melons firmly in place. They can be washed and worn up to twenty-five times, so that's just a buck sixty per wear (neimanmarcus.com)!

COMMANDO TAKEOUTS

I'll be honest—I like Takeouts because of the darling Chinese takeout packaging. And perky little devils that they are, they'll make you look so egg fu *young*! Position them along the outer curves of your favorite underwire bra and prepare to have your cups overfloweth—by an entire cup size (barenecessities.com).

NUBRA SILICONE BRA CUPS

Think of the strapless-dress utility of Le Lusion Plunge Cups with the volume perks of Takeouts. This silicone bra snaps together in the front so it will work for all styles except a plunging neckline. The added thickness is like an instant boob job. Hint: Be sure to apply them to a clean, dry chest sans moisturizer or body oil, unless you want your NuBra to slide onto your lap during a black-tie dinner. But if they do, just smile and say, "I didn't know chicken cutlets were on the menu." (macys.com or nubra.com or beauty.com)

- -

BUTT *seriously . . .*

When someone says you look like you lost weight, don't shut them down with a negative crack about yourself to deflect being put on the spot. Yes, sometimes it's more irritating than flattering, but if you can just say "Thanks, love!" you'll own it.

- -

carson confession: RETURN OF THE PINK PANTHER

A friend of mine, Bridget, suffered from breast cancer three years ago, which required a double mastectomy, radiation, and chemo. Being a nurse and one of the bravest women I know—and also a dead ringer for a feisty blond Gidget—she was a champion from the start. She got a great wig that looked as close as possible to her former hair and powered through her treatments. But her body was another story. Since losing her breasts and having implants, all she wanted to do was hide in something comfortable. For a whole year—including New Year's Eve—I couldn't get her to part with the same black North Face zip-up fleece she wore daily. But the annual Pink Ball at her local hospital was coming up in October, which was also her birthday month, and we decided to call a breast intervention. Her hair was back, and so was her health, so all she needed was a good excuse to show off her chest again. We found a pretty, supportive bra that gave her a great shape under the bold pink shift dress she chose to go with the theme. Whether it was the dress that showed off her great legs, the lacy underwire bra she was wearing underneath, or knowing that she was celebrating her second year of remission feeling okay with her body, her gutsy spirit came back. She still jokes that it was "my coming-out party . . . for my new tits."

SWIMSUIT SOS

Shopping for swimwear isn't ever a day at the beach, is it? I have the same anxiety making itty-bitty Speedo selections in hopes that someday I'll bump into the Croatian water-polo team. The goal is to choose pieces that are comfortable and supportive but in flattering cuts that make you feel sexy. So you don't get dressing-room burnout, make a plan of attack by zeroing in on styles you know are going to do yourself a favor.

BE A WRAP STAR

You can't go wrong with a crisscross front that works like the upper half of a wrap-front dress. The ruching in the fabric smoothes out any excess jiggle, and this style often has a built-in bra for added support. Keep it simple by choosing a full-piece suit in a dark solid. I love the site swimsuitsforall.com because there are so many super-affordable, stylish options that incorporate everything from color blocking to mesh, making a black suit look anything but basic.

GO THIGH HIGH

The mantra "the more you cover, the better" isn't always true. A higher leg opening is always going to be more flattering than a lower one. Despite it showing more skin, the cut makes your thigh look longer and therefore thinner. The good news is, this eighties Jane Fonda leotard cut is back in a big way (minus the pink and purple stripes). Go for the burn!

Tszuj Do It . . . Put a massage, body wrap, or other blissful body treatment in your iCalendar. It might seem silly, but taking the time to indulge your body can do amazing things to reset your self-perception.

AVOID THE "MOM SUIT"

Like mom jeans, there's a mom one-piece to avoid, and it usually involves crazy prints and too-long tankini shirts, which are meant to camouflage but do just the opposite. A smaller, well-structured tankini with a waist panel or one with a tapered handkerchief cut gives the best lower-tummy control when layered over a full-cut bottom. Tropiculture has a variety of sexy, ultraflattering tankini styles with built in tummy-control lining (amazon.com, overstock.com, sears.com).

SKIRT THE ISSUE

If you feel more comfortable taking the emphasis off of your hips or tush, try a one-piece that has a light skirt over it, so it has some movement (thicker, longer styles will just add bulk). Lands' End makes a number of styles; they aren't necessarily fashion-forward, but they're figure flattering and great quality (landsend.com).

> Getting my lifelong weight struggle under control has come from a process of treating myself as well as I treat others in every way.
>
> **OPRAH**

SWIMSUIT BRANDS TO SWEAR BY . . . NOT SWEAR AT

Aerin Rose

Anne Cole Collection

Bond-Eye

Freya

Jantzen

Lands' End

Lisa Curran

Old Navy

Miraclesuit

Panache

Tara Grinna

Tropiculture

Victoria's Secret

ViX Paula Hermanny

BUTT *seriously . . .*

Rinse your bathing suit in cool water after every swim or dip in the Jacuzzi, because chlorine and hot tubs stretch out those nice, taut fibers in the fabric. A stretched-out suit is like a soggy eggroll: It can't hold all the good stuff together.

DRESS FOR
your shape

Now that you have the right foundation for your clothing, how do you dress to bring out your best features? Wardrobe stylist Ashley Loewen, my makeover partner in crime on *Carson Nation*, has you covered. Here are some common body types she works with and her tried-and-true tricks.

HOURGLASS

"If you have a balanced figure like the hourglass, accentuate that God-given waist. This can be done with a wide belt or form-fitting top that skims your curves. A wrap dress would be perfect for you. By the way, anyone can fake an hourglass shape by creating a waistline. Pair a wide belt or leather wrap belt over a tunic or thin sweater. Try a peplum top or a form-fitting blazer that has a little nip in the waist."

APPLE

"Most women with an apple figure tend to throw on an oversize top and think that they are concealing their tummy. Wrong. The larger the top, the larger you actually look. Find a top that is flowy but not oversize. Or try a structured jacket with a shift dress to show off your legs. If you carry weight in your middle, a skinnier leg and mid-rise jean with a fitted rear will give you a lengthening effect without tummy spillage. Pair those jeans with an elongating tunic or fitted blazer, and all the focus will be on those great gams."

Says figure-flattering guru Ashley, "I've been lucky enough to dress hundreds of women, and the beautiful thing is that we come in all different shapes, sizes, and love different styles." Amen.

BUTT *seriously . . .*

If you're wearing a fitted item on the bottom, your top should be looser, and vice versa. While a head-to-toe fitted look can absolutely work, rarely does everything tight or everything loose look flattering. Unless we're talking about David Beckham.

TRIANGLE

"If you have a triangle body shape, your shoulders are smaller than the widest part of your hips. Try a top with a bold pattern or add a statement necklace to pull people's eyes up. Slenderize your bottom with denim or leggings in black or charcoal, with a ballet flat, cowboy boot, or bootie. Leggings should have some heft to them. They're going to give you that support and be like a body shaper. I like leggings from Express (express.com), Simply Vera (available at Kohls.com), and Nordstrom's Zella 'Live In' Slim Fit Leggings (nordstrom.com)."

INVERTED TRIANGLE

"If you have an inverted-triangle body shape, your shoulders appear wider than your hips—almost the exact opposite of the triangle. To rebalance your body, wear a solid color V-neck top with a long necklace and a midi-length, patterned skirt that adds curves. Remember to keep all pattern and extra fabric to the bottom half of your body."

SQUARE TORSO

"Create a column of color up and down the middle of your body for length. I like a navy blue trapeze top and dark wash skinny jeans plus a sleeveless vest for contrast. You can also do this with color blocking—wearing a dress or top that is black only on the sides to create the illusion of a slimmer silhouette. Both strategies have an elongating effect. The slimmest part of woman's body is generally just below the bustline, which is why the empire waist can also work wonders for narrowing a torso. Skip tentlike, baby-doll styles and opt for a structured seam underneath the bust and ruching on the bodice."

It's OK to want to look and feel your best. It's OK to work at being attractive, whatever that means to you. And it's also OK to not expect to be defined by that. It's OK to be powerful in every way: to be big, to take up space. To breathe and to thrive.

CLAIRE DANES

TEN do's AND don'ts FOR DRESSING longer AND leaner

Instead of squeezing yourself into a waist trainer that crushes your internal organs, or berating yourself for not being your target weight, why not simply dress slimmer and let yourself off the hook? The slenderizing "dos" are green-light looks that flatter every body. The "don'ts" on the right make me hear that screeching brakes.

DO'S Whoa, Have You Been Doing Pilates?	DON'TS Whoa, Have You Been Doing Dunkin'?
Monochromatic looks (they don't have to be black). Even white can be slimming worn from head to toe.	Cutting yourself in half with contrasting colors that change at the waist or hips
Nude stilettos, kitten heels, strappy sandals that fasten below the ankle bone, toe cleavage	Ankle straps that interrupt the length of your leg (a cankle creator), big square toes, chunky heels
Structured bag that is either long and narrow or tucks in naturally at the indent at your waist	A wide bag with a flare-out bottom that hits you at the largest point of your hips (aka saddlebag sabotage)
Skinny jeans with a straight leg, slight flare, or boot cut that will balance out thicker thighs	Skinny-to-the-ankle jeans that increase calf-to-thigh drumstick ratio
Long, thin dangly earrings that elongate your neck	Wide, tight choker that shortens your neck
Short or long coat with princess (aka hourglass) seaming in back and darts in front	Mid-length coat to cover your tush (it will shorten your torso and widen your thighs)
Pants with medium-size, close-set butt pockets placed high enough to give a little lift	Pants with small, low, spread-out butt pockets that drag your derriere down

I'm the recipient of a lot of backhanded compliments . . . where people are like, "It's so nice that Mindy Kaling doesn't feel she needs to subscribe to the ideals of beauty that other people do." And I'm like, "I do subscribe." They're like, "It's so refreshing that Mindy feels comfortable to let herself go and be a fat sea monster!" By the way, I run and work out. It takes a lot of effort to look like a normal/chubby woman.

MINDY KALING

BUTT *seriously* . . .
Whether you're petite or curvy, a garment that's well structured on the hanger is going to hang better on you than one that doesn't. It's an easy equation: Good shape on the hanger = good shape on you.

Tszuj Do It . . . Splurge on a body cream
that makes you feel delicious. My favorite is Jo Malone Wood Sage & Sea Salt Body Crème (jomalone.com), but it could be as simple as Palmer's Cocoa Butter from the drugstore.

DO'S Whoa, Have You Been Doing Pilates?	DON'TS Whoa, Have You Been Doing Dunkin'?
Fluttery chiffon sleeves or structured cap sleeves that wing out as if they had extended shoulder pads (like little carports for your shoulders)	Circulation-cutting cap sleeves at the widest part of the upper arms, or spaghetti straps that show armpit cleavage or enlarge the upper arms
V-neck and crisscross tops that draw your eye down and inward	Crew-neck and boat-neck tops that pull your eye horizontally
Rayon-nylon-spandex leggings with seams down the back and panels at the sides, to minimize the thickness of the leg	Thin cotton leggings that look like tights and have no structure, showing every lump and bump in the upper leg and bum

BUMP IT Up!

Ginger Zee is chief meteorologist at ABC News. She and I share a close mutual friend, but we've also bonded many times on set. It's so nice to see someone so cheerful and gorgeous that early in the morning! Ginger recently popped out her first baby, a little boy named Adrian, and wanted to share some style tricks about how she dressed her mommy-to-be body.

"As I morphed into a house, feeling great in clothing wasn't all fun and games. But I have learned that for me, looser is better. While I totally embraced my bump, going a size up and feeling free in my clothing was liberating and less revealing. One of my least favorite looks is the belly-button reveal that so many women inadvertently don as their navel protrudes. I like fabrics that mask this or dresses and tops that are cut in a way that gives that poor thing a little room to breathe!"

"The biggest secret I've learned is that rental maternity is the way to go. We all know we don't want to hold on to an entire wardrobe that will never fit again. And even if it did fit, if I decided to have another baby, the style would change. Utilizing the awesome companies out there, like Le Tote, Belly Bump Boutique, and Mine for Nine that rent maternity wear, especially for special events, is almost as genius as the people who came up with those concepts in the first place. Wish I had thought of that first!"

Last Halloween, Ginger fearlessly dressed up her bump as Humpty Dumpty, a basketball, an avocado pit, and Mr. Potato Head. Next time around, I'm going to suggest a Fabergé egg.

My smile is my favorite part of my body. A smile can make your whole body.

SERENA WILLIAMS

Strike A POSE

A woman once asked me on a talk show how to hide her belly when she's posing for photos. I said, "Get a puppy!" Seriously, if you hold a puppy right there, everyone will just look at the dog. In cases where cultivating a canine is not available, I've always had good luck with the following body moves. Say *fromage*!

DO THE TORSO TWIST

Stand perpendicular to the camera lens so your shoulder is pointing toward the lens, Miss Diva. Turn your upper body and face toward the lens while keeping your lower half in place. Got it? Twisting your torso into the camera is a universally flattering angle and also helps when you're being photographed while seated. Leg lengthening tip: If you're sitting down, point your knees at a 45-degree angle away from the camera.

GET HIPPY WITH IT

Rest one hand on your hip (only one!), whichever one feels better. Turn to the lens and tell your cameraman to make it snappy so you don't have time to overthink it. It should feel like a fluid process: twist your torso, square your shoulders, smile, click, Instagram.

BE SELF-CENTERED

Don't be shy about using other people as camouflage when you take a photo. If there are a couple of people around you on either side and you're in the middle, you wind up getting framed by the group, which always looks good. It also hides arm flab. Eventually they'll catch on to it and ask, "Why are you in the middle all the time?" and you can coyly say, "Because I'm the Beyoncé, that's why."

DO THE MISS UNIVERSE BEVEL

Place all your weight on your back leg, then drag your front leg into your body, give a little knee bend with that leg, and stay on your tiptoe. It's the classic beauty-queen bevel, and it does the job every time.

GET PHOTOGRAPHED FROM ABOVE

Always have the person taking the photo be at a higher angle than you, rather than crouching and shooting upward. If they take the picture from the ground up, it will have an *Alice In Wonderland* "Eat Me / Drink Me" effect, where everything will look disproportionately larger and chins you never knew existed will appear (no, no, no!).

DO A PINUP POSE

Remember all of those voluptuous belles with fuller figures from the forties and fifties? Make like Rita, Jane, and Marilyn and lean slightly forward with your arms while you suck in your waist and twist that torso. Or face away from the camera and turn around coyly with a hand at your hip. Classic pinup poses might feel awkward, but those gals knew how to work their body angles rather than hide under a beach towel.

BE A FLASHER

It's always beneficial to have the washing-out effect of a camera's flash because it blurs the imperfections so you look smoother and wrinkle-free. Also consider ambient lighting. Anytime you're being photographed indoors you should face a window rather than stand in front of one. Backlighting will highlight your silhouette and every lump and bump. It'll also make your hair look flatter. In outdoor shots, always face the light source, so your photographer has his or her back to the sun.

You're a human being, you live once and life is wonderful, so eat the damn red velvet cupcake.

EMMA STONE

carson confession:
MARSHA, MARSHA, MARSHA!

Raise your hand if you love Marsha Mason! If you don't know Marsha, she's a fierce, St. Louis–born, four-time Oscar nominee and Broadway star. I was hosting a show on Channel 11, and Marsha was doing a promo for a project of hers. I thought we were ready to roll the cameras, but the producers said, "Hold on; we have to get Marsha Mason set up here!" Marsha had brought her own professional lighting for her segment. I thought to myself, *Now that's an old-school Hollywood professional, bringing her own lights to Channel 11.* She had ring lights and standing lights, which worked so great because they created a diffused glow that warmed up her face and hair. Marsha must have known that whether you're indoors or outdoors, strong light coming down on the top of your head, like a french fry under an infrared light at McDonald's, is never going to be flattering. It can create those kind of downward shadows that show bags and everything else we don't want the world to see. What can we learn from Marsha? You don't want uplighting or downlighting, but surround lighting (like surround sound). Translation: If you're at a party, get out from under those kitchen ceiling lights and find a seat near that gorgeous lampshade that will illuminate you at eye level. Yes, you can wear the lampshade, too, if the Shiraz keeps flowing.

BODY CONFIDENCE *Tips* FROM A SHOWGIRL

Even though I've ridden horses my whole life, I never gave much thought to my posture until I started working on *Dancing with the Stars*. I'd see the dancers and the way they sashayed about with their outturned legs and pointed toes—even just walking over to get a snack from the fridge—and think, *Oh my God, you're so talented.* I asked one of my closest friends, Kym Johnson, who is not only a *DWTS* alum but a former showgirl for the Sydney Review, to share some of her personal confidence builders:

SAY: "TITS AND TEETH!"

"When I used to be a showgirl, this is one of the terms we'd whisper to each other before performances when we were dragging. Essentially, it's 'Fake it till you make it.' If nothing is going your way and you just can't pull it together, smiling wide and projecting your chest automatically gives you a more secure presence, because it pulls your shoulders down and back."

PRETEND YOU'RE AT LAX

"When I stand, I keep my head high and my tummy pulled in, but I pretend I'm carrying a heavy suitcase in each hand. That way you keep your shoulders down and relaxed while still having a confident carriage."

FIND A "FAUX" FOCAL POINT

"When I'm dancing solo, I look just above everyone's heads. It appears as if I am looking right at them and projects natural poise, since my chin is raised, but I don't get stuck locking eyes with someone who might throw me off my game. You

Does being in a Kym Johnson and Olivia Newton-John sandwich make me an honorary Aussie? Hopelessly devoted to both of you gals!

can do the same thing when you walk into a party or crowded work event and don't know anyone. Focus just above everyone's heads and you'll instantly exude confidence."

DON'T GET WINTER-BODY SHOCK

"Waiting until just before summer to work out can sap your confidence because you feel like you have too far to go to get back in shape. Make exercise a year-round activity so you don't feel out of control. Make it a hobby, like hip-hop, Parkour, SoulCycle, or Zumba, that is engaging enough that you aren't constantly checking the clock. And get a fitness buddy to keep you motivated. That principle also works for us on *DWTS*."

WELCOME TO *booty camp!*

No longer is the tiny tushy the epitome of a fierce body—and why should it ever have been, anyway? Consider maximizing your natural ass-ets with some strategic moves that build strength and get those endorphins going. High and round, ladies, high and round!

TWERK IT, GIRL

While my own twerking skills are still in development, I know more than a few women who swear by their "twerk-outs." Invite your girlfriends over and check out Keaira Lashae's Twerk Tutorial on YouTube's DailyBurn. Rev up with some green juice or kombucha or your bev of choice, lace those high-tops, and start twerkin'. Just move mother's antique Ming vases before you begin—because once the booty pops, it don't stop.

GRIN AND BARRE IT

If you're more of a traditional fanny firmer, hop on YouTube and try the BarreConcept Ultimate 20-Minute Barre Exercise Workout by Barre-Concept creator Emma Newham. Why Emma? Besides her tip-top form, I just love a long-haired ginge with an ambiguous UK accent who says "tuck" (which sounds like "look") and "You gettin' that shake on?" Note: If your legs are rattling like an 8.5 on the Richter scale, you're doing it right.

Tszuj Do It... Why wish for a thigh gap when you could wish for toe cleavage instead? Declare it National Shoegasm Month. You don't need a teetering stiletto to make your leg look lean and mean. The fab factor could come from being in snakeskin or metallic or a cage bootie that looks fierce dressed up or dressed down.

GET A FITBIT

Forget about getting fit—this step-counting bracelet is all about fashion, people! It actually looks like a casual-cool cuff (I personally love the Flex in Slate). For a chichi version, Tory Burch makes an adorable Double-Wrap Fret Bracelet in neutrals like Bark / Aged Gold and French Gray / Silver. Aim for ten thousand to twelve thousand steps per day, and it'll light up when you've hit the mark. Hooray, time for gnocchi! One of my girlfriends who works full-time and has four children still finds the time to get in her tush-toning steps, so no excuses. Her secrets: Park up the hill and walk to pick up your kids at school, sneak in a twenty-minute morning or evening walk with the hubs, and choose stairs over elevators and escalators. Oh, and shopping requires a lot of walking, so shop more! It's good for you (fitbit.com).

CARSON'S CALORIE CONVERTER

- **Fighting other women at a three-hour sample sale = 275**

- **Running a half mile in heels to Crush-cakes before closing = 130**

- **Opening a bottle of chardonnay = 15**

- **Opening a bottle of chardonnay with your teeth = 42**

- **Having sex = 300+**

- **Having sex with yourself = 100**

- **Having sex with yourself and Joe Manganiello = 200**

- **Breaking in ski boots around the house = 66**

- **Lugging fur and vegan coats to the dry cleaners = 22**

- **Car dancing to Drake = 42**

- **Cyber Monday shopping = 10**

- **Rolling your husband over so you don't have to hear him snore = 24**

- **Resealing your Carrara marble counter-top = 55**

- **Waxing your child's unibrow for picture day = 18**

- **Turning pages of this book = 2**

Feeling a little lighter? Must be all that dead weight you dropped while reading this chapter. Ditching old habits and self-critiques is a sign that you're taking responsibility for your own happiness. And happy equals hot. Without all that negativity clouding your vision, you'll finally have the freedom to see yourself in a fresh, objective light—the way the rest of the world does. If you aren't able to fully embrace all the body boosters we discussed, give it a chance to marinate.

carson confession:
FROZEN: LET IT GO, LET IT GO!

Y'know that feeling you get when your cheek goes numb from sucking on a pop? That's the science behind CoolSculpting. I know, it sounds bizarre, but it's sort of incredible. If you're able to stomach the cost (around $700+ per zone, with an average of two to three zones), this procedure promises to freeze 25 percent of your fat cells permanently and has no downtime after the procedure. You can even do it on your lunch break—which is probably less painful than listening to your coworker's latest adventures on christianmingle.com.

A dear friend in her forties did CoolSculpting to get rid of what she jokingly called her "sandbar." It was a stubborn lower tummy patch of flab that was left over from four pregnancies, plus two poochy humps on either side of her belly button. While she was getting her fat frozen off, she caught up on the latest season of *House of Cards* on her laptop while enjoying some Pinkberry (weren't you curious?). She said the cold wasn't bad after the first few minutes, and it didn't hurt. The vacuum was the shocker: It had a weird pulling feeling when the machine first grabbed her target spots. For a few weeks after, she felt numbness in the area, but it wore off, and a few months later, she wore her favorite bikini again on her fifteenth-anniversary trip to Mexico, which she was proud enough to post on Facebook. She got such great feedback that her hubs asked for CoolSculpting for his love handles and upper back flab as his belated anniversary present. No one should feel pressured to lose their flab; it's yours and you can hug it and love it and shake it to Shakira. But if it's been bugging you because it won't disappear despite regular exercise, or if you're allergic the gym like I am, it's worth hopping on the Polar Express.

7.

Really, I WOKE UP Like THIS!

Pour yourself a drink, put on some lipstick, and pull yourself together.

ELIZABETH TAYLOR

- -

DIM THE LIGHTS, PLEASE.

My hands are clammy, my pants are tight, and I'm locked in an embrace with a mysterious Russian wearing her sequin number in her favorite color, *peeer–pul*. It seems like just another day in Los Angeles. But alas! I am performing live in front of nineteen million viewers on *Dancing with the Stars*.

Allow me to set the stage: I am a swashbuckling pirate, donning black Latin pants—the high-waisted, ass-enhancing variety—a glue-on beard I could never grow in real life, smoky eyes, and spray-on abs, which I requested even though I wasn't shirtless or even wearing an open shirt. *"But I'll know they're there!"* I begged the spray-tan team.

Speaking of bronzed abs, I must divulge that on *DWTS All Stars*, I heroically volunteered to apply self-tanner and moisturizer to the abdominal wonderland of Gilles Marini, French actor and eye candy best known for his sizzling naked shower scene in the critically acclaimed *Sex and the City* movie. It was like massaging Crisco on a lobster shell. Had. To. Share. But I digress. Back to the show!

My whole career, I had costumed other people. Now, onstage, in front of what seemed like the entire world, it was my turn to be transformed. In rehearsals it never felt great. I was a Caucasian guy trying to cha-cha. But with the hair and lighting and outfit and synergy onstage, it all clicked. As I landed my "death spiral" with love interest Anna Trebunskaya, in which you elegantly mop the floor with your partner (okay, maybe they only gave that move to *Maxim*, but I did something equally suave), little old

Just so you know, I slept in my beard that night.

almost-Amish me had morphed into Academy Award–winning, multitalented acting phenom Johnny Depp in *Pirates of the Caribbean: On Stranger Tides*! Plain and simple, the right wardrobe gets you primed for the role. I didn't feel like I was ready to get the job done until I *looked* ready to get the job done. And it took a village— a glam squad, if you will.

Think about someone you know who always looks "on." She probably has a glam squad of her own. She may not be a natural beauty (did I ever tell you natural beauty is totally overrated?), but no one would deny that she's attractive, polished, and totally in control. You bump into her at the grocery store, and her hair is frizz-free, freshly highlighted, and trimmed in a flattering shape. Even in harsh Walmart lighting, her eyes are bright and her skin glows. At work, at the gym, in the pickup line, her style is perpetually on point . . . and so are her gel nails. (Beyotch.) Now ask yourself, *Why can't I be her?*

My answer is: Why *can't* you? I can tell you firsthand that it takes a lot to make even the most famous people camera-ready. Not only have I been part of glam squads on more television shows than I can count, I've gotten up close and personal with hair and makeup teams on all the talk shows, backstage at the Oscars and the Miss Universe Pageant, and behind the scenes on *RuPaul's Drag Race*. There are the hair teasers, the frizz tamers, the shine stoppers, the airbrush makeup whizzes, the chin-hair pluckers, the pants pinners, the boob lifters, the under-eye-bag magicians, the lash-fringe fabricators. A complete beauty school battalion! There are even people who will put eye shadow on your scalp to make your hair look fuller on your thinning front part (my secret is taupe eye shadow). Without those glam squads, celebs would look *just like us*! So why not consider the inverse and realize that with a little tszuj-ing, you can look *just like them*!

The bottom line is, all of us need a constellation of star helpers to keep us powdered and groomed like an Aspen ski slope. And they don't have to cost big bucks if chosen carefully and creatively. It's all part of giving yourself a style checkup. Sure, you get a physical, a mammogram, and dental cleanings once or twice a year. But how about having your wardrobe, makeup, and hair evaluated regularly by experts, then creating a plan of action to maintain the goods?

DO YOU NEED

A GLAM SQUAD INTERVENTION?

Answer the questions below to see where you stand.

1. I don't know any tricks to avoid major fashion emergencies.

2. I often strike out when I get help from department-store salespeople.

3. I wouldn't bother consulting a stylist to help me pick out clothes or accessories.

4. I'm never quite happy with my hair color or cut.

5. I wash my hair every day without fail.

6. I can't seem to get control of my grays.

7. I pluck and pencil in my own eyebrows.

8. I use eyeliner and shadow but don't know the secret to a smoky eye.

9. I use blush to shape and contour my cheeks.

10. I use highlighters on books, not my face.

If you answered yes to one or more statements above, it's time to broaden your beauty horizons. Everyone is a work in progress and can use a little TLC from talented gurus.

If I did not have my glam squad, you would not believe how shitty I would look right now.

JULIA LOUIS-DREYFUS

HOW TO FIND A *free* STYLIST

You'd be shocked at how many glam squad resources are available to you without dropping a dime. All it takes is a little sleuthing.

START SCOUTING

Almost everybody lives within fifty miles of a great store. Even if you're not going to scoop up an entire wardrobe, there are generally tastemakers in any town who can be your inside track to what trends are happening now. Make a short list of your favorite boutiques in your area, and find out what days the owners or high-level associates will be in the store. The most helpful people are generally at the helm of those places, since they have the most stake in keeping happy customers. Let them know what you love and what works on your body so they get a feel for your style and can pull things in advance and set them aside for when you're ready to pop in.

WORK THE BIGGIES

At big department stores like Bloomingdale's, Neiman Marcus, Saks, Macy's, and Nordstrom, personal shoppers abound—and they're taking on young and busy clients, not just your rich Aunt Hildie. Even independent retailers like J.Crew have caught on. Their complimentary Very Personal Stylist program gives you access to haute tips on iPad style stations and allows you to book a face-to-face with an in-store stylist. They'll track down tough-to-locate sizes and styles for you and help you craft a fab wardrobe geared to your shape. You have access to them twenty-four hours a day, every day. Which, let's face it, is more face time than you give your family.

CHALLENGE 'EM

It's time to change up the dynamic if you're used to walking into a store, fiddling your way through a few racks, and saying, "Oh, no, just browsing!" when someone offers to help you find something specific. Why not challenge them by saying, "Actually, Linda/Naomi/Christy, I'm looking for something that is going to blow my mind with how easy it is for me to wear and feel good in. No special occasion . . . I just want to be dazzled." Step back and see if they surprise you.

DON'T BE INTIMIDATED

She could be a personal shopper at Neiman Marcus or a trusted style maven who owns a consignment store in your town. You may be thinking, *She's not going to give me the time of day*. But nine times out of ten, these people are warm and gracious and want to help. It goes beyond just selling you something. So check your intimidation at the door. Be candid and say, "Gosh, I don't know what I'm doing, but I have this occasion coming up and I would like to look x or y way."

- -

BUTT *seriously* . . .

Macy's has rolled out a program called My Stylist @ Macy's, for which you can book free stylist appointments online or by phone. They'll help you with everything from wardrobe boosters to wedding wear to buying foolproof gifts for family and friends.

- -

MAKE A PERSONAL CONNECTION

A lot of major retailers want to build a clientele. If you feel comfortable with the associate who helped you and feel they've done a great job, give them your contact info and grab their card. When you build a relationship, they'll be more apt to have you on their mind when new inventory comes in and will call you when they predict a good fit. Have her send you photos of the items beforehand so you know what you're getting into—literally.

COME PREPARED

It'll save you both time if you arrive at your appointment having thought about a few basics: your lifestyle, colors and styles you like, your body type. Also think about what your style goal is (revamping your fall wardrobe? Cancan-ing on Carnival Cruise Line?). It gives your personal shopper a good starting place. If you're working with a department store, you'll likely have a minimum of two appointments per year with your personal shopper as maintenance, but you can squeeze in far more than that. Why not? She works on commission, so keep on coming!

It's weird at my age that, you know, people think that I dress well and that I look good. I think it's kind of neat that I'm in my seventies before somebody says, "Oh, she's great on the red carpet and she's a fashion icon." Moi? I hardly think so, but I've learned to fake it.

JANE FONDA

GLAM SQUAD GUEST STAR:
Ashley Loewen

You've already met rockin' wardrobe stylist Ashley Loewen in the last chapter. What you may not know is that she's an ace at performing fashion emergency triage, too!

COMFORT IS KEY

"No director likes to call 'Cut!' because of a wardrobe malfunction. So I try to make sure everything is perfect before we start shooting. I think the biggest thing we forget about when shopping or putting on an outfit in the morning is to ask, 'Do I feel comfortable?' Is this skirt too short, shoes too high, jacket too tight? If you feel the slightest bit of discomfort, *stop*! Find something else. An uncomfortable outfit can ruin your day."

If there's any friend I'd call in a clothing crisis, it's Ashley. Copy all of the little tricks she uses on her clients as if she were your own stylist.

JUST ADD FROSTING

"I always remind clients that being on-trend isn't copying Cara Delevingne or the latest issue of *Vogue*. It's knowing what works for you and your body and incorporating pieces of the moment to make yourself look on-trend. Accessories will make a simple, timeless outfit trendy in two seconds and keep your costs low. Think: a new bag, shoes, a statement necklace."

GET A LIFT

"I am a huge fan of a heel. It changes the way a woman stands. But if it's too tight on the toes, my television host could be miserable. So I make sure I purchase moleskin in different thicknesses to give extra padding where it is needed to keep her feet happy when they swell after ten hours in heels. Oiling your feet to slip into a shoe helps, too. Nonskid pads for the bottom of shoes are also key. They add traction to the bottom of a slippery smooth-surface shoe so you can strut with confidence or dance the night away at a wedding."

STAY IN PLACE

"Topstick is my lifesaver. It's essentially double-sided tape that is great for hiding bra straps, keeping a lapel down or ties in place, or making sure a low top doesn't overexpose anything by accident. You can also take a top that has a boat-neck shape, or a dress that has at least one-inch straps, to the tailor to create bra-strap holders. It's very inexpensive but saves you the stress of having your straps fall down."

DON'T SWEAT IT

"You may not consider yourself a serial sweater, but it's amazing how people wind up sweating more than usual in high-stakes events. I'll attach Garment Guard Disposable Underarm Shields to their tops so they don't even have to worry about it."

PUT A PIN IN IT

"Large safety pins are a must in a stylist kit and can be used to extend a necklace length. If you are curvy and love a necklace and it is hitting you too high on your neck, you can still wear it: Add a large safety pin to cheat the length. Just make sure your hair is down so you don't see the evidence!"

- -

BUTT *seriously* . . .

I learned a lot about fashion emergencies while judging the Miss Universe Pageant. For one, hairspray isn't just for hair! Keep your gown from clinging to your derriere by spraying the inside of the fabric. Beauty queens even spritz it on their faces (eyes closed!) to set their makeup and over their deodorant to prevent white-stripe dress drama. PS: The girls use "firm spray" to keep bikini bottoms from riding up, too—which is great for gripping if you enjoy pole dancing to Britney, like I do.

- -

sourcing
ONLINE STYLISTS

More than ever, there are resources on your phone, laptop, iPad, and even your Apple Watch that will make getting dressed more streamlined. It's easier than online dating—even the breaking up part!

everywear.com

The styling app Everywear is like having your very own magic-fairy fashion editor at your disposal. How's that for retail therapy! After swiping and uploading to establish whether you have their thirty key basics in your wardrobe, you'll get a free half-hour, one-to-one styling session (via text chat) with a stylist on how to shop your own closet. They will have a virtual version of your closet from what you've uploaded, and they will incorporate new pieces from chosen online retailers. These go in your "try-on box" that gets shipped to you; you can send anything back in seventy-two hours. The app is free, but their premium membership, available in select cities, entitles you to a special house call from a stylist for $150.

keatonrow.com

How Brit-tastic is this name? I love that before you even sign up, styling app Keaton Row gives you a slew of looks to browse on their site, compiled by various editors whom you know by name—from "date night" to "9 to 5" to "desk to dinner." Sign up, and your personal stylist will create a multipage lookbook for you based on your free styling-session convos. Don't dig what she's selected? Get rematched with a new stylist. Your purchases are logged into your "wardrobe," so your stylist can help you gradually build a curated collection, which gets updated each season. Keaton Row also has its own line, available through Saks, Shopbop, and Les Nouvelles.

stitchfix.com

The Stitch Fix app is unique in that it truly tailors finds to your personal budget. Your first step is to take a quiz that helps their stylists create a personal style profile for you. From that, they'll pop five pieces to you per month by mail. Keep all five and you nab a 25 percent discount on everything. They do charge a stylist fee of $20, but it gets put toward your future purchases. Your shipment will have style cards with assembled outfits, shoes, and accessories mixed and matched so there's little room for error. Users post real reviews of the service and recent purchases. Helpful? Totes!

thenetset.com

While it's not a personal styling app, The Net Set is certainly an app about personal style. Think of it as a social network for shopping, with its own "Style Tribes." It features live feeds on what clothes, shoes, and accessories are trending among the millions of stylish users in The Net Set community. Browse others' comments on lusted-after items and check out the items they curate. It's like overhearing dishy conversations at a dinner party!

trunkclub.com

If your man is a prisoner of pleated-front khakis, sports jerseys on date nights, or "dad" jeans with—gasp—white sneakers, get thee to Trunk Club, pronto. This online styling service pulls together looks for your man and ships them out (in a "trunk"—get it?). Free shipping, free returns, zero excuse not to try. They also have outposts in Chicago, Dallas, D.C., L.A., and N.Y. for custom stylist fittings. Stay tuned for a women's version, coming soon. Let me get on that.

> One day I decided that I was beautiful, and so I carried out my life as if I was a beautiful girl. I wear colors that I really like, I wear makeup that makes me feel pretty, and it really helps. It doesn't have anything to do with how the world perceives you. What matters is what you see.
>
> **GABOUREY SIDIBE**

Tszuj Do It . . . Book a girls' night in on glamsquad.com. Their party package offers twenty-minute dry-styling and makeup refreshers so you can get all your ladies together and each enjoy a touch of glam without the full hour-long makeup application or forty-five-minute blow-out. Because time's a tickin'—the Chippendales are coming in five.

like Uber FOR BEAUTY!

These traveling-beauty-team apps let you choose your service, time (last-minute bookings are welcome), and location. Your home, your job, your gym, your hotel, your tax attorney's office? Done! While most on-demand services are limited to select cities, you can bet these businesses and more like 'em will branch out fast.

BEAUTY BRAND	What It Does	Where to Find It
Manicube	Fifteen-minute manicures and twenty-five minute dry pedis at the office (its most popular locale), private parties, and retail spaces; manicube.com	Boston, Chicago, New York City, San Francisco
Glamsquad	App booking with under an hour's notice; bridal services, discounts for friend referrals, bulk-buying, promos for signing up to their newsletter/ e-mail, e-mail gift certificates; glamsquad.com	Los Angeles, Miami, New York City
Priv	Haircuts, blowouts, massages, makeup, spray tans, manis, facials, weddings; gopriv.com	Austin, Hamptons, Los Angeles, London, New York City, Orange County
Style Bee	Updos, makeup, blowout + makeup, updo + makeup, add lashes for $10. Airbrush makeup is an additional $20; stylebee.com	Los Angeles, San Francisco, San Jose
Stylelisted	Hair, makeup, and hair + makeup; stylelisted.com	Chicago, Los Angeles, New York City, Washington DC
StyleSeat	Hair color, haircuts, makeup, nails, weaves, and extensions; styleseat. com	Atlanta, Austin, Baltimore, Brooklyn, Charlotte, Chicago, Columbia, Dallas, Denver, Houston, Las Vegas, Los Angeles, Miami, New York City, Orlando, Philadelphia, San Antonio, San Diego, San Francisco, Savannah, Seattle, Tampa

GLAM SQUAD GUEST STAR:
Cory Bishop

Cory Bishop is a celebrity makeup artist and brow-whisperer to the stars at Anastasia Beverly Hills. He knows everything about creating perfect brows and making up a fab face. If you can't make it to 90210 to get glammed up by Cory, hop in his imaginary makeup chair for a virtual one-on-one:

Renowned makeup artist and fab friend Cory has a favorite motto: "Confidence is something that is so easily lost, making someone feel beautiful is the best way to give it back." Cory, my eyebrows are waiting for you!

BE LOYAL

"People think, *Okay, I have an event in two days; I'm going to get my brows done with whoever is available.* But it's important to choose one brow stylist and be loyal. It takes awhile to grow into the style that they're working toward. If you see different stylists each time, they all may have different ideas of what shape your brows should be, and you'll wind up undoing the work that was done. Do your brows deserve an identity crisis?"

TAME YOUR TWEEZING

"The biggest problem I see is overtweezing. Women want a lift in the eye area, so they pluck underneath to get that lift. If you keep tweezing from underneath your brow and just rely on hair growing in from above, you're going to make your brow too high, which gives that "surprised" look. Thinner brows can emphasize a large nose or a wide lower jaw and can even make close-set eyes look closer if they're tweezed too much in the middle."

START STENCILING

"Unless you can hide out for a month while you let everything grow out, do it gradually. That's why I love the stencil program we use at Anastasia (anastasiabeverlyhills.com). You choose a stencil that fits your face shape and is a little fuller than your current brow. Use a pencil or powder (if you're oily) to fill in that stencil shape. Whatever falls outside of the stencil is fair game to tweeze. Once hairs grow into that stencil, move up to a fuller stencil, until you've graduated to your ideal full, high arch."

Tszuj Do It... Scare yourself silly at celebswithnoeyebrows.com.

GO TWO-TONE

"I always put two colors on the brow. You can tell a person is wearing brow color when they're wearing only one shade, because it makes it more painted on. Hair isn't all the same color, even the smallest hairs on the brows. You want to create the illusion of a shadow against the skin that is created by hair. Shadows tend to be a bit lighter, so you go a little lighter than your root color. Add in detail with a slightly deeper color."

FOLLOW THE GOLDEN RATIO

"Eyebrows control the symmetry of the face, and studies show that symmetry is directly correlated to how attractive we are. That's why if you try to re-create a brow look that works for someone else—whether it's Megan Fox or your best friend—it won't work. Here's how to use Anastasia's golden ratio so your brows are in proportion to your unique contours, making your features look balanced, feminine, and youthful."

Ratio 1

Draw a straight line from the center of your nostril up to your brow. That's where the brow should begin. If your brow starts too wide, it can make your nose look wider and eyes look even closer set by emphasizing the inner corners of your eyes.

Ratio 2

Measure the diagonal from the outside corner of your nostril to the outside corner of your eye. That's where your brow should end. When people overtweeze they lose that end, and as you grow older, hormones signal the brow hair to stop growing. As your brows get shorter, they can make other facial features look larger.

Ratio 3

Draw a diagonal line from the center tip of your nose to the center of your iris. This is where the highest point of your brow should be. This takes into consideration the relationship of the size of your nose to the size of your brow. If you have a larger nose, a larger brow will look more balanced.

- -

BUTT *seriously* . . .

Try Latisse on bald patches of your brow, or dab on the men's formula of Rogaine. It's a paste; the women's formula is a thinner consistency and harder to control (i.e., accidental unibrow).

- -

CORY'S FABULOUS FACE TIPS

Foundation, concealer, blush, and highlighters are so hard to get just right, especially if you're buying your products in drugstore packages without having the opportunity to color-test them first. Read Cory's makeup mandates to avoid looking like you popped a Valium and started playing with your kid's Crayolas:

START SPONGING

"I work in HDTV and if I miss a foundation line on a client's face, it shows. That's why I love applying foundation with an edgeless, rounded sponge, so it always looks blended and natural. I show clients what I mean by putting foundation on a mirror with a brush (looks streaky) and a finger (high and low spots, so makeup doesn't look even). When you stipple or "bounce" with a sponge, it blends and pushes the color out as you apply to your own skin, so you get a more even application."

SKIP SHEER FORMULAS

"I don't recommend sheer foundations for anyone. You can always wear a full-coverage foundation and 'sheer' it out by mixing it with moisturizer or primer for a smoother application. You'll get more product for your money. Hourglass makes a nice oil-free foundation that gives coverage but feels lightweight, Stila Stay All Day Foundation & Concealer has a great shade range that isn't pink-y, and Make Up For Ever Ultra HD is also getting a lot of buzz" (available at sephora.com).

BUTT *seriously* . . .
If you like to "try before you buy," hit Macy's Impulse Beauty section. Touch, test, take votes! You'll get help from an independent beauty adviser (i.e., someone who won't push one brand in your face) in picking products.

BUTT *seriously* . . .
Try Cory's favorite foundation tool, the Beautyblender (beautyblender.com). The colored ones are fun, but the white sponge won't ever leach dye when you clean it. Wet your sponge and wring it out before applying.

SAVE YOUR MASK FOR THE BALL

"The reason people will put foundation all over their face is because it's the wrong shade and they want it to look even. With silicone-based foundation in the right shade, you only need to use it where you really need it. I color-match with the neck because it has the least amount of sun exposure, and there's less redness because there are fewer blood vessels. I always tell people, 'When in doubt, go lighter.' Redness, pimples, and hyperpigmentation will darken your skin, so lighter shades will even things out. Or buy two shades and mix them. Then you can warm it up with bronzer."

DISGUISE DARK CIRCLES

"We're taught to go one to two shades lighter with under-eye concealer, but when you do that, you draw more focus to under-eye skin, which looks crepey as women age. Plus, light concealer reads as white on dark under-eye circles, which mixes to make gray. I always tell my students that gray is the first color I was told to use when I learned how to make zombies! Go with an under-eye concealer that is exactly your skin shade or even a bit warmer. Orange turns blue circles brown, which will turn tan with your lighter foundation layered over it, while a concealer with yellow-green undertones combats reddish-purple circles. Steer clear of pink concealers if you have any red: You'll look like you had an allergy attack."

USE THE RIGHT BLUSH BRUSH

"The biggest mistake women make with blush is using the tiny brush that comes with the package. I recommend a soft, domed shape for a diffused, natural look. It's really old-fashioned to 'shape' your cheeks with blush. Now we're using contouring and highlighting, and the blush is just for warmth. I always think of blush as an aura where you have a glow about you, not where people say, 'Oh, I like your blush.'"

BUTT *seriously* . . .

Primers have come and gone . . . kind of like pagers! Skip the expense if you know that your foundation has a silicone base—the active ingredient in primer—which won't break down with oil.

STROBE YOURSELF

"As much as it sounds like a young trend, strobing is actually ideal for women as they age. It is basically contouring, but only with highlights. Contouring uses cooler colors, which on a mature woman can look sunken, while highlighting brings features forward and makes cheeks look fuller and more youthful. Try a fluffy eye-shadow brush for powder highlighter, because you just want to target the cheekbone. Just avoid glittery formulas. Broken-up glitter highlights texture, which makes crow's feet and acne more visible. I use a lot of liquid highlighters because liquid looks skinlike and adds dewiness. Anastasia launched an Illuminator highlighter with mica that is milled so finely, it looks liquidy, which is the best of both worlds."

BUTT *seriously* . . .

It's not oil in makeup that makes monster zits. Oil just enhances the bond between dirt and dead skin, which is what triggers breakouts. That's why keeping up with your skin-care regimen is key.

CORY'S SECRETS TO SEXY LIPS AND EYES

"When I was an artist and learned how to draw faces, the hairline, browline, lash line, and lip line were really the only four lines we'd draw; the nose is just shadows," says Cory. "When those four lines are in proportion, it's like smoke and mirrors because acne, wrinkles, and age spots fade away a little more." Sign me up! Now that you have an eyebrow plan (and will get hair help later in the chapter), let's focus on Cory's secrets for your orbs and your kisser.

LUSCIOUS LIPS

"I like lip liners because they strengthen that all-important lip line. Their paraffin base helps them hold up well and look great with a glossed lip. The key is to blend so it fades in. Otherwise you could look Joker-esque. Use a lip brush to blend so it can get smooth without bleeding into fine lines around the lip. If the first swipe of the brush removes too much color, layer more. Otherwise, it'll come right off with your first sip of coffee."

INTRIGUING EYES

"The reason we wear shadow and liner, dating back to the Egyptians, is to make the lashes look stronger and fuller and mimic the shadow created by a full set of lashes," says Cory. Let's get lining, shall we, Cleo? Julius and Mark are waiting.

Line the Inner Rim

"You want your liner to really touch the base of your lashes. That's why lining the inner rim along the waterline has become so popular. The line looks more invisible, but your eyes look more open and attractive."

Layer Up

"If you have a twelve-hour day and need to take it into night, give it staying power. Always use the lighter shades first and layer in darker ones. I see people do the reverse and wind up with a lightened lash line when it needs to be strong. Go over your eyeliner with a brush and powder. If it comes off, you need more."

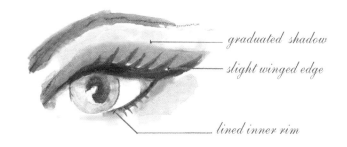

graduated shadow

slight winged edge

lined inner rim

Wing It Right

"I often see people bring the line down too much on the sides when they wing their liner. The last thing you want to do is accentuate the droop. If you want to wing out your liner, curl your lashes. Look at where your outermost lash hits, and make that your stopping point for your wing. This isn't a 747."

Try a Smoky Eye

"The traditional smoky eye works for every eye, regardless of size, face shape, or age. It accentuates the lash line and doesn't need to take anything else into consideration. You want to go darkest closest to your lash line and lighter as you go up, like a horizon."

- -

BUTT *seriously*. . .

At birchbox.com, you can have customized beauty booty delivered to your doorstep. How fun is that? If you fall in love with what they send you, full-size versions of products are for sale on their site.

- -

- -

Tszuj Do It. . . Kris Jenner travels with

her own makeup mirror with professional lighting so she always looks impeccable on set. How do I know? I've seen it! Get your own portable light-up makeup mirror, like the Sephora Collection Bright Up Close LED Makeup Mirror for $26 (sephora. com).

- -

GLAM SQUAD GUEST STAR:
Hector Pocasangre

Hair makes a powerful first impression. Forget about eye contact—it's all about hair contact! I called on my friend, star hairstylist Hector Pocasangre, for his dos and don'ts on putting your best follicles forward. Let's hair what you have to say, Hector!

HECTOR'S HAIR DOS AND DON'TS

Do: Tell your hairstylist what you don't like about your hair. "It's much more valuable information for us than saying what you do want. People want everything! Not realistic! We'd rather use the process of elimination. If you say your hair is too brassy or you don't like the layers, we can fix that. The more you can articulate, the better the result."

Don't: Bring in photos of hairstyles on people you look nothing like. "Otherwise you'll just be disappointed that the end product doesn't look like the photo. If you have fine hair, pick a celebrity that has fine hair. If you have a pinkish complexion, don't bring in a photo of Ariana Grande. Face shape similarity is crucial as well."

BUTT *seriously . . .*
Lighten up! The older you get, the more you need highlights. Dark hair accentuates dark circles under the eyes, while lighter tones soften them and make wrinkles less noticeable.

Hector's a total tease—when it comes to hair styling, that is. He creates everything from glam pompadours to voluminous clip-in looks fit for a queen on *RuPaul's Drag Race*, fashion shows, and more.

Do: Stretch out appointments with a spray-on color. "My clients with grays definitely benefit from a temporary touch-up. I like Style Edit Conceal Spray because it doesn't drip or run off when you sweat. Lightly spray a few inches away from the hair."

Don't: Go superblond. "If you look at a child's hair that is natural blond, there are streaks and variations in tone. When you go too light or overhighlight, there is no variation, and you end up frying your hair."

Do: Use dry shampoo to avoid overwashing and to extend a blowout. "Section off your hair so you can spray it onto your scalp, not your hair. Big Sexy Hair goes on wet, and you have to dry it a little bit. I use it on set a lot because it gives great volume. R+Co Death Valley Dry Shampoo smells so good and doesn't get white and powdery. It's good if you're a more-is-more person and will spray it all over your hair. It might sound funny because of the infomercials, but Bosley BosRenew Volumizing Dry Shampoo makes a very light and clear dry shampoo that is ideal for finer hair. It doesn't weigh it down and is great for brunettes because dry shampoos take the luster out of dark hair."

Don't: Let your stylist put product on your roots. "Not if you want to extend your blowout! Never use oil on the ends, either. I use Evo Easy Tiger Straightening Balm when hair is wet and only use a little on the ends. R+Co Chiffon Styling Mousse is great if you have fine, limp hair and need volume. It gives some bend in the hair if you are getting waves or using a curling iron."

Do: Use toner. "I recommend professionally applied toner, or use a shampoo to tone your highlights between appointments. I like Davines Alchemic Shampoo or Clairol Shimmer Lights Shampoo. Choose the Blonde & Silver formula to cancel out brassiness in blond hair, and the Brunette & Red formula to enhance the luster of brown hair."

Don't: Assume gray = no style. "I have a lot of clients who want to age naturally. The way to do it is to use keratin treatments, since gray hair is coarser and prone to dryness, and not let it grow out too long. Cut is so important. You want to have texture for short looks and a strong shape and movement for longer styles, so it doesn't look wispy."

carson confession:
LASSIE, COME HOME!

A famous colorist I worked with once told me, "You need some lowlights because your hair is very blond." He came to my home and used a color called Golden Walnut. *Gee*, I thought, *this looks a little (gulp) dark*. Within minutes, Golden Walnut turned my head maroon, like Sharon Osbourne black cherry (gorgeous on her, not so much on me). "Don't panic!" he said. "We just have to strip out all the color and start over." It took nine hours, and I was almost in tears. At the end, my hair looked like the collar of Tom Hardy's coat in *The Revenant*. I'm talking full-on border collie. Hence my baseball-cap period. I learned the hard way to make sure the person you're working with has a clear picture of what you do and do not want. Unless your goal is to break the Internet on the "People Who Look Like Their Pets" gallery.

Tszuj Do It . . . Spoil yourself with a monthly "Barfly" membership at DryBar, which for $75 plus tax gives you two blow-drys per month, plus a free birthday blowout. You also get discounted prices on additional blow-drys if two just won't cut it (thedrybar.com).

HECTOR'S HAIR GEOMETRY LESSON

Attention, pupils: Next time you have your hair cut, ask your stylist to analyze how your hair works with your face shape. Here are Hector's hints:

ROUND FACE

"Steer clear of bangs, which will make your face look pudgier. Go for a layer that is cut just below the cheekbone, like a long curtain. It will hide a little bit of cheek area to accentuate the nose and the inside of your cheekbones."

SQUARE FACE

"Your face has a lot of angles, so a blunt cut is going to look harsh. You'll want to layer it up to create more softness around the square. You don't want to overaccentuate the jawline. A side-swept bang would be perfection."

HEART FACE

"A rounded bang softens the wideness around the top of the head and accentuates your pretty cheekbones and eyes. You're one of the few people who can pull off a short bob or a pixie, so go for it."

OVAL FACE

"You can get away with everything, honey. This is the shape most stylists try to create, because it has symmetry and balance."

LONG OVAL FACE

"The grown-out-bang look looks great on you, but keep everything just past the shoulder or higher. When your hair is too long it drags your face down and can even have a witchy look."

carson confession:
ON BORROWED WINGS

Hair is the one thing people never want to change. People could morph every other thing about themselves, but the hair is the hardest to part with. Get it? Part? Oh, never mind.

I once worked with a woman named Donna who had what I called Rip Van Winkle Syndrome. It was as if she fell asleep in high school and woke up forty years later with her same exact Farrah Fawcett feathered wings from the mid seventies. It was a classic case in which she wanted to hang on to her younger self, and High School Hair was her fountain of youth. For her, that period represented the best years of her life, when she was eighteen and sassy and sexy and had all of these wonderful memories.

But she was now in her fifties and living in a time warp. I had to convince her to let go of the past by getting excited about the present. She was back in the dating pool after being newly divorced, which was a big transition and demanded a new look. We convinced her to clip those feathered wisps, warm up her ash-blond color, and try a supercute, swingy cut that flattered her great bone structure. It made her look ten years younger. Kate Jackson and Jaclyn Smith would have definitely given her two guns up!

GLAM SQUAD GUEST STAR:
Marco Pelusi

My friend celebrity hair colorist Marco Pelusi doesn't just have DNA in his hair, he has hair in his DNA! Marco comes from a family of hair dynamos and worked in-house developing hair colors for various manufacturers. He's the perfect person to quiz y'all on hair, so here goes:

TEST YOUR HAIR IQ WITH MARCO!

1. How long does hair grow, on average, each month?
- *a.* ¼ inch
- *b.* ½ inch
- *c.* ¾ inch

2. What's the correct way to shampoo?
- *a.* Get a nice big lather going with a high-PH product
- *b.* Use a shampoo with a low PH and lather very little

3. When should you shampoo before getting color?
- *a.* The day of—color absorbs better on clean hair
- *b.* The day before—you want it clean, but not too oily
- *c.* Two days before—the more natural oil you have, the better

4. When is the ideal time to shampoo after getting color?
- *a.* Twenty-four to forty-eight hours later, to rinse out excess residue
- *b.* Forty-eight to seventy-two hours later, so the color can oxidize

Mega-talented Marco owns Marco Pelusi Hair Studio in West Hollywood and has his own line of products. It's located next door to the Christian Louboutin store— can we say dangerously good combo?

5. The amount of shampoo and conditioner you use should be the size of a:

  a. Trojan

  b. Hilton sister's engagement ring

  c. Chocolate gelt

6. Where on your hair should you apply shampoo and conditioner?

  a. Shampoo on the roots, conditioner on the middle and ends

  b. Shampoo on the roots and middle, conditioner on the ends

  c. Shampoo all over, conditioner on the ends

7. What should you put on your hair before jumping in a pool?

  a. Bathing cap, especially so blondes don't go green

  b. Conditioner or gel to provide a moisturizing barrier

  c. Water so the chlorine rolls off and doesn't penetrate

8. If your hair looks brassy, the best color-toning shampoo to use is:

  a. Purple

  b. Gold

  c. Brown

9. Should you cut before you color, or color before you cut?

  a. Always cut before you color so your ends don't look fried

  b. Always color before you cut so the ends look fresh

  c. Doesn't matter, but cut first if you're taking off a lot

10. What is demi color?

  a. A six-to-eight-week semipermanent option that deposits color without giving you a root line

  b. An ombré-like technique that tints the upper or bottom half of your hair

  c. The shiny, jet-black hue that once slayed Bruce Willis and Ashton Kutcher

Answer Key: 1. b, 2. b, 3. c, 4. b, 5. c, 6. a, 7. all of the above, 8. a, 9. c, 10. a

FIFTY SHADES OF GRAY? NO WAY!

Use Marco's color formulas to tame those silver streaks.

BLONDIES GOING GRAY . . .

Highlights to camouflage and brighten

Plus demi color for toning out gray

BRUNETTES GOING GRAY . . .

Highlights to camouflage and brighten

Plus lowlights to bring back natural color

Plus demi color for toning out gray

**BLONDIES ALREADY
ONE-THIRD GRAY . . .**

Single process, with or without toner

**BRUNETTES ALREADY
ONE-THIRD GRAY . . .**

Single process, with or without toner

BUTT *seriously* . . .

Whether you highlight, tone, or single process, you need a specialized shampoo that won't strip out color. My faves are Marco Collagen Color Guard Hair Care (marcopelusi.com) and Aloxxi (amazon.com).

WINTER, SPRING, SUMMER, OR FALL . . .

Which season are you? Follow Marco's formula to ensure your hair and skin are in harmony:

Winter: Dark eyes, olive skin, or deep African American skin tones and dark hair, or brunettes with pale or blue-toned skin

Avoid: orange and red hair colors

Stick to: cooler colors like ash brown and espresso, true reds, and violet tones

Spring: Golden blondes and brunettes with warm skin undertones

Avoid: ice blonde or ashy brunettes

Stick to: warmer hair colors like honey or strawberry blond

Summer: Pale blonds with light eyes and fair skin undertones

Avoid: golden, yellow, or strawberry blond

Stick to: cool colors like ice and ash blond

Fall: Warm browns, redheads, and red browns with ruddy or warm undertones, or lighter African American skin tones of toffee or mocha

Avoid: light blond, ashy colors

Stick to: copper, chestnut, auburn

My dearly departed friend Joan Rivers always got her blond just right. I can almost hear her now, saying "Carson, stop it some more!"

HI, maintenance!

Optimize your time by booking in advance and in tandem. Book facials and waxing at the beginning of the week so your skin can recover, and book hair at the end, so you have a weekend of fab hair.

I couldn't have said it better, Coco Loco! Now let's bring it on home in our last chapter with more amazing wisdom from all of the iconic, beautiful, intelligent, amazing, funny, fabulous, and unapologetically strong women I've been with.

By "been with" I mean women I've seen on television, appeared with on television, or canoodled with in the VIP lounge at the Emmys!

What did you think I meant?

SERVICE	How Often	Helpful Hint
Brows	If you're growing your brows to a certain shape, you should see your brow specialist every two to three weeks. If you're maintaining, you can get away with every four to six weeks.	Say you're on board with the stencil program. Don't buy a stencil that's too bushy (Cara Delevingne) if you're pencil thin (Pamela Anderson) at this point. You'll have too much to fill in with powder in the interim.
Body waxing	Every two to six weeks, depending on how *Planet of the Apes* you are.	Tend Skin (tendskin.com) rocks for ingrown-hair busting and razor bumps. Put it on your hubby!
Haircuts	Every two to three months for longer styles; six to eight weeks for cropped cuts.	Continue getting your hair cut if you're growing it out, but do it every *other* time you think you need a trim.
Highlights	Every eight to twelve weeks; the longer you can wait, the better condition your hair will stay in for the long term.	Stretch out color by using toner at the halfway mark. Hit the salon at six weeks for a tone and wait another six before highlighting again.

I don't understand how a woman can leave the house without fixing herself up a little, if only out of politeness. And then, you never know, maybe that's the day she has a date with destiny. And it's best to be as pretty as possible for destiny.

COCO CHANEL

SERVICE	How Often	Helpful Hint
Single process	Four to six weeks for a touch-up if you're 50 percent gray, and three to four weeks if you're 70–100 percent gray.	If you use box color between visits, buy a lighter shade. Your stylist can easily darken a lighter shade but has to bleach/highlight when it's too dark. Only do the part, an inch right and left of your part, and along your hairline.
Gel or shellac nails	Every two weeks. Don't peel those babies off, or your real nail will get stripped down when you do. Plus, it'll just look like you got hungry.	Since gel and shellac can be super drying on your nails, it's a good idea to let them go naked every few months. Apply Earthly Body Miracle Oil (amazon.com) on nails and cuticles.
Facials	Once a month is golden, but who has time for extractions that often? If you can't swing it, once per quarter is fine.	For extra credit, get a peel or micro-dermabrasion for some serious glow. Try the end of summer or in winter when dead skin is at its peak.

8.

Just Between
US GALS

Style is knowing who you are.

GORE VIDAL

- -

THERE ARE A NUMBER OF WAYS I COULD have ended this book. I could have written a one-act play, starring Karlie Kloss and Joaquin Phoenix, about the rise and fall of the gladiator sandal. I might have penned an algorithm for how many accessories one needs to properly offset a ginormous pimple, a tattoo of your ex-boyfriend's nickname, or skunky-looking highlights. Or I could have made a list for you, now that we're such good pals, of fashionable films, from *Funny Face* to *Foxy Brown*, that we can watch when I come over to your place to drink your wine and eat your non-G.M.O. popcorn.

But I think you've heard enough random tips from me and my style fairies to fill a deck of Cards Against Humanity. So I thought I'd mix it up by spending our final moments together dishing about and getting the dish from some of my favorite fashionable women (and one beautiful man) in the universe. What makes these people so fabulous, and why should we get pulled into their gravitational field? The common denominator is that as a group, they possess three qualities I adore in fashion and in life: humor, confidence, and rule-breaking bravado.

THE *dream* TEAM

Cher-ing is caring! The following four stars are no strangers to the red carpet, but I'd like to shine a li'l more light on their iconic roles in the world of fashion.

CHER

Let's start where it all began: Cher. I've been a Cher fan all my life—make that *in utero*. I probably was in my past life, too, as a gilded iguana. I discovered Cher on TV when I was five years old and, like any gay child of the seventies, I would pull up my plastic Playskool chair and sit in front of the tube, mesmerized by her Bob Mackie dresses (not to mention her oversize earrings, which looked to me like small planets orbiting the sun). For the uninitiated, Mr. Mackie was known as the "Sultan of Sequins" and the "Rajah of Rhinestones," and he created evening wear with a jeweler's precision. When Cher slipped on one of Bob's sheer, belly-button-revealing creations,

it was pure envelope-pushing artistry. Add to it a dramatic black-feathered headdress that would make Alfred Hitchcock's birds fly the coop in jealousy, and all I could think was, *Who is this goddess, and how can I be like her when I grow up?*

I first met Cher in the era right after *Will and Grace* in the late 1990s/early 2000s when, let's face it, fashion wasn't that fabulous. We were in a dimly lit club for a movie premiere, and I was wearing a leather jacket, lace-up boots, and a bolo. Cher probably was, too. But that night, fashion didn't matter, because our love-at-first-sight moment was beyond fashion! We locked eyes from across the room, and before getting the nerve to smile back, I looked over my shoulder to make sure she wasn't smiling at, oh, I don't know, Jack Nicholson. When I looked back at her in disbelief, mouthing, *Me?* She mouthed back, *Yes, you,* and signaled me to come hither. Could I be the Will to her Grace? Yes, yes, I could! I was in the Cher Circle of Trust! I had an opportunity to interview her for a fashion magazine weeks later, and even in her hotel room, wearing a black bandanna and velour loungewear, she was real and owned it. Years later, I dedicated *Off the Cuff,* my men's style book, to Cher. She wrote me a beautiful thank-you note, on Cher stationery. Yes, that note is prominently framed in my bathroom. It makes my eyes twinkle every time I tinkle.

Cher is the original Kim Kardashian. Her dark hair, her big eyes, her full eyebrows, her glossed lips, and her body-con clothes have always been otherworldly. At the peak of her career, she was on the tips of everyone's tongues because she was outspoken and glamorous and approachable. She was someone that you would idolize, even before you recognized her talent, because her look was so powerful. When it comes to fashion, Cher was and always will be a risk-taker, a button pusher, an independent thinker, and someone who doesn't give a f—.

Sometimes you need a little bit of "Cherattitude" in your wardrobe to push your personal style. I'm not suggesting you should subject yourself to a full-body bedazzling, but let her no-holds-barred vibe encourage you to unleash your own version of a bolder you. It could be as simple as trading in your typical understated bag for a chartreuse one, your Tiffany heart bracelet for a leather cuff, your baseball cap for a fedora. In Cher's world, you don't take one thing off before walking out the door . . . you put one more thing on. Her message is: Don't be a wallflower. Go over the top every once in a while—whatever that means for you.

There are fashion icons throughout history, like Cher, who immediately give us a visual when we hear their names, whether it's Audrey Hepburn, Ali MacGraw, or Sarah Jessica Parker. The stars you don't remember are the ones who don't have their own brand of style. But when you see someone like Diane Keaton, whom I was lucky enough to spot on a plane a few weeks ago wearing a felt fedora, fingerless gloves, a peplum jacket, and Buster Keaton pinstripe pants with a double RL belt, you get it right away. Her appearance isn't just an extension of her personality. It makes a statement: *I'm here, I've cultivated a look that works for me, and I'm happy not following the crowd.*

SHARON STONE

Sharon Stone is part of this visually unforgettable cadre of women. I met Sharon when she was presenting an award for the Creative Arts Emmys. I remember sitting in the second row and feeling my jaw drop when I saw her come out in all her cropped-hair glory. She's a "movie star" like Katharine Hepburn, and possesses an old-school glamour and swagger you don't often see anymore. We bonded as fellow Pennsylvanians, and I must have given her my phone number, because a couple of weeks later, while I was getting a mani-pedi at Blooming Nails in Manhattan, I got a call from a blocked number. "Hi, Carson, it's Sharon." I paused. Sharon, Sharon, Sharon . . . OMG. "Sharon Stone?" This is the fun part of my job. I won't tell you the rest of what Sharon and I talked about, because I don't remember it, and you know we didn't wind up in bed, anyway. But I did wind up at the *Lovelace* premiere, and she wore a white minidress with gold grommets and a bouffant. I brought a date with me that night, and after noticing our Carson-Sharon-Pennsylvania reunion he said, "Wait, you know her?" I smiled smugly, fiddling with my cuff. "Yes, we're besties."

Sharon is one of Tinseltown's greatest bombshells, but she isn't the archetypal actress with long, full hair, curves for miles, and big boobs. She's a handsome woman—and I mean that in the most flattering way. She's striking and unusual, not your cookie-cutter blonde. When I think of Sharon, I instantly see her in her white dress in the chair with her legs crossed in *Basic Instinct* (and then they uncross and I see something I don't want to see), but you get my point. Her ice-princess combination of short, slicked-back hair, simple makeup, diamond studs, and mono-chromatic knitwear looks confident and effortless. I think that image of her is consistent with how she dresses in real life. Famous for wearing a Vera Wang ball skirt with her then-husband's white Gap shirt to the Oscars one year, and a plain charcoal Gap turtleneck with a Valentino trumpet skirt another year, Sharon was a trend trailblazer. Yes, other people have done menswear, and yes, other people have had short hair, but at that time, she was really bucking tradition in Hollywood when everyone else was wearing Nolan Miller gowns and *Dynasty* hair. Sharon proved that mixing high and low wasn't just cool, it was the definition of fearless fashion, and it was totally relatable. That's a way of thinking anyone can adopt—from pairing a simple T with a satin tuxedo jacket, or a lacy chiffon blouse with distressed jeans.

Summer Lovin'

CHARLIZE THERON

Charlize Theron is another bombshell who taught me a lesson I try to impart to each and every woman I work with: Don't gild the lily. I realize not all of us lilies look like Charlize's South African variety, but sometimes less really is more. My first encounter with Ms. Theron was when I interviewed her on the red carpet at the Oscars. It was the year she took home the Best Actress statue for *Monster,* and all eyes were on her. Charlize's champagne Gucci gown glittered like a true Hollywood starlet's, but there wasn't a part of her body that was overdone. Her hair, in simple forties-style waves, didn't overshadow her long diamond earrings, and those earrings didn't outshine her diamond cuff. Her lips were pale, allowing her eyes to hold the drama. Everything was in balance, so that when you took in a head-to-toe gaze, all you saw was a glittering, golden body, soon to take home another golden body that she could put on her mantel. By the way, she let me hold her Oscar, and it was like cradling Goldfinger's newborn baby!

The next time I saw Charlize was at a nightclub in Vegas. She called me up to her VIP section, and when I got there, I realized she was the most casually dressed person in the club. Yet somehow, in just jeans and a T, this style chameleon possessed the same glamour that she did on the red carpet. Her clothes looked like a second skin—without looking as tight as one—and she had just the right amount of tszuj: a nude heel, a simple bangle, some lip gloss, and mascara. Done. As fun as it is to pull a complex outfit together, sometimes my feeling is *Why complicate it?*

Dreamboat

TOM FORD

Speaking of complicated, you have probably guessed by now that my one and only real fashion crush is my pretend husband, Tom Ford. There's nothing tricky to his look, except for looking gorgeous. He has a simple uniform: a black jacket and a white button-down that's often unbuttoned at least to his nipples, the same five o'clock shadow, the short-short hair. He embodies a distilled, singular glamour, just like the pieces he

designs. Maybe it's a beautiful hide in suede, or the thickest cable-knit cashmere. Tom teaches us, just by breathing, the importance of splurging on pieces that are luxurious but understated, the kinds of pieces you'll put on year after year because they don't date themselves (though *I would* date his clothes. . . . I'd probably take them to Barneys for a ladies' lunch, followed by a Broadway show).

Our love affair began with me admiring Tom from afar. When he was designing for Gucci, I was working for Ralph Lauren in Milan. I remember him at the Gucci runway shows, emerging from behind the curtain to give clapping audiences his elegant wave. I was sure he was waving only at me (there *was* eye contact, okay?). And then I never saw him again—just like most of my dates. Men. Can't live with 'em, can't kill 'em.

The turning point came at a gala at Cipriani for the Tenth Accessories Council Excellence Awards. Tom was ducking out of the back entrance with Naomi Watts, I think for a ciggy, and I was doing the same (that was back when people smoked, remember?). It was raining, which made the whole thing even more cinematic, with the three of us huddled under a doorway just to stay dry. And it was probably the most spectacular three-way of my life. Oh, right, it was the only three-way of my life. Anyway, Tom was in his trademark beautiful black velvet dinner jacket and a bowtie, with a black-and-white silk scarf tucked effortlessly into his lapel. Caveat: It was one of the only times when his shirt was fully buttoned. I thought, *Darn it, here I am four inches away from you; why can't I get a visual inventory of your individual chest hairs?* Tom was like the grown-up version of my childhood crush, Burt Reynolds. There's a reason

I saw *Smokey and the Bandit* seven times. I like you, Sally Field, I *really* like you . . . but it wasn't you!

The next time I saw Tom was at the Rainbow Room at the Top of the Rock for his Black Orchid fragrance launch. Jennifer Hudson was singing, and it was this huge party. I don't know how I got invited, but I was there, sipping cocktails high in the sky. I saw him walking through the crowd, making his rounds in that same debonair black-and-white silk scarf, but with an unbuttoned shirt this time. Finally! I think I drooled in my cosmo. Then he actually stopped and—wait for it—hugged me and *kissed me on my left cheek.* If I could have lived without my head, I would have had it removed and hermetically sealed in Baccarat crystal. Since that wasn't possible, I eventually washed my face, and Tom Ford's DNA sadly went down the sink.

I didn't run into my love again until I popped into Bergdorf's one spring day to check out the new Tom Ford shop. Unfortunately, as we've all experienced with our on-again, off-again paramours, this was an unattractive bump-in. Like, epically unattractive. I had just been to my old-school, Upper East Side allergist, who had "cured" my sinus infection by sticking a wire through my ear that came back out through my nose. It was all very 1934. I was swollen and gross looking; I hadn't shaved the four hairs on my chin, my hair had no product, and I was wearing Lilly Pulitzer shorts and a white piqué polo that made me look like a lesbian golf pro. As I was bent over, fondling an $8,400 pair of alligator loafers, I heard a voice behind me say, "Carson?" in a *raspy, gravelly, movie-star kind of way.* I popped up, still holding the shoe, and froze. "Tom Ford, oh, my God, Tom Ford. What are *you* doing here? I'm just looking at shoes. Oh, I look so terrible." He was like, "No, I like your stubble." He liked my four golden whiskers? He liked my four golden whiskers! Then he disappeared in the blink of an eye.

Tom, if I mean anything to you, anything at all, you'll name one of your lipsticks in your next Lips & Boys collection after *moi.* Just thought I'd put it out there, since I'm so very discreet and so completely not obvious.

Seven Wonders
OF MY WORLD

Still with me, girls? Now it's time to hear from a group of women (and one inimitable and iconic gender-bender) who inspire me for so many reasons. They're a mix of ages and ethnicities, just like my Tinder queue. You'll want to swipe right on all of these gems!

CYNDI LAUPER

Not only is Cyndi a fashion maverick who happens to know a great deal about the history of fashion (I think she would have been a great teacher at FIT or some other fashion college, because she has such zeal for the subject), the Emmy-, Grammy-, and Tony-winning legend is a leader for social change. We met when I hosted her *True Colors* tour, traveling to cities all across America to strengthen the alliance between the gay and straight communities. Since then her

passion for ensuring that everyone can show their "true colors" has morphed into championing for the eradication of LGBT homelessness. It's something we have worked on together for a number of years. I mention all of this because it is this sense of wanting everyone to be proud of exactly who they are that resonates not only in Cyndi's music but in her approach to fashion—and I love her for it.

CK: Cyndi, of all the women I know, you have never *not* dressed with edge.

CL: I've always been a bit of an outsider, and being an artist, it's a comfortable place for me fashionwise and lifewise. I think dressing with a little bit of flair is romantic. I grew up in the fashion age, and my family was in the fashion industry. My grandmother was a seamstress and my uncle was a pattern maker, and everybody sewed. Course I didn't! But I went to The High School of Fashion Industries and studied fashion history, and I also worked in a vintage store. When you're surrounded by it, you start to understand what looks good on you. Not everyone has the time to learn, but there are wonderful things that you can steal from looking at old editions of *Vogue* and checking out the fashion from the thirties and forties. It's good to learn your history, because when you go shopping, you see that influence on the racks. You can always take from vintage and mix it with what they're doing today to make your look more interesting. If you see a vintage jacket you love but it doesn't fit just right, get it tailored. If the interior is worn, use the pattern to make a new one. That's what we did in my family.

CK: What are your favorite clothes to wear?

CL: I think the most exciting and dangerous and hard to wear is Comme des Garçons because some of it is so amazing and it's for a particular body shape and it's just so out there. I also love Italian movie-star dresses. Those look good on me. I always battle with my weight, because I could very easily be a chubby old Italian woman. I'm short-waisted and wear peplum styles because it gives an hourglass shape. That's why I used to wear corsets. It makes your waist go in more and gives a good silhouette. But I take a photograph first. There are some things that look great in the mirror, but in photos, it's not so good. If it looks good on the iPhone, then wear it. If you see it bulges here or there, put a pair of Spanx on and try it again. See if you feel comfortable. You should wear clothes that empower you. That's the most important thing.

CK: I've seen all the "true colors" of your hair. Just last week it was pink.

CL: I like pink. I did it before Pink became a singer. As you get older you can have any color hair you want, as long as you keep it soft. I like to play with color schemes. If I wear all beige, everything should be beige, even my hair. I did that for *Redbook* magazine once. It was a Mother's Day piece and they asked us to wear all white. So I spray-painted my hair white, too. I was so excited,

but when I got there, no one else looked like me. I kind of did look like a freak. But you've gotta get into the art of it.

CK: What would you say to women who are in a hair rut but are just too busy to change their hairstyle?

CL: As you get older, you don't have just one job anymore. Everyone is multitasking up the wazoo, especially women. So the time you get to spend on yourself is minutes. But make the effort. You have to take a photograph of what the shape of your face is. If you have cheekbones or a round face, you want to follow the line of your jaw and not have it drag down. Go and try different wigs on with different hairdos and see how you feel. Or get a little hairpiece that your hairstylist can always put in for an updo. Like those ladies on Virgin Atlantic. I love those little buns they use. They're cute, and they look pretty real.

CK: How has your makeup evolved, "time after time"?

CL: In the eighties my makeup was war paint. But as you get older, you can't overdo it because it looks too harsh. You can do any style on your face if you do it soft. You can learn all kinds of tricks about makeup by studying looks from history, like photographs by Richard Avedon and Irving Penn. Check out the old movie stars, particularly women who are your age and have your face shape. Try it when you have a second. I had to because I was in the public eye. But you don't wear makeup for other people. You wear it for yourself.

CK: What are your must-have beauty products?

CL: I use a lot of Tracie Martyn. It's organic and pretty pure stuff, and when I put it on I see a visible difference right away, not over time. It moistens your face and softens your skin, and that's all I care about, and that it's not going to kill me. I use her serum and her activator and those square collagen sheets that you put on and they look like a hockey mask. I also think it's important to find the right primer. I noticed in Japan that the women didn't wear a lot of makeup but they looked flawless. When I was in the department stores there I noticed they use a lot of primers and a smoothing veil that you put on under makeup. I also like those round pink sponges you buy and soak 'em and ring 'em out. You put your makeup on your hand, then use the sponge to put it on your face. It makes it look smooth and covers everything.

ALYSIA REINER

I first met amazing Alysia at a film screening in New York, and what struck me about her is that she is every bit as much of a force as "Fig," the warden she plays on *Orange Is the New Black* (except she's sooo nice, supports women in the arts, and is hell-bent on making the world a kinder, gentler, greener place! Don't throw me in jail,

please!). An award-winning actress, pioneering indie filmmaker, and passionate humanitarian and environmentalist, Alysia is a blend of earth mother, old soul, and street-savvy chic. No matter how glammed up she looks in photos, the down-to-earth feminist is quick to remind her daughter that pictures in magazines are not reality but "painted to make people look extra pretty." Except for photos of Carson. I look perfect every single day.

CK: How do you look like a million dollars on the red carpet without dropping a mil?

AR: Here's the thing about a red carpet look: You only wear it once, so I love to borrow designer pieces for a night. It's also a super eco choice and I am a certified green gal. For noncelebs, you can do that with sites like Rent the Runway and wear something amazing for a fraction of the cost. I also believe in spending money on classics, like a timeless pair of men's-style black trousers that make you feel amazing, a designer bag that will be in style forever, a tuxedo like the one Yeohlee made me for the Season 3 premiere of *Orange Is the New Black*, an incredible pair of loafers or Mary Janes, a cashmere sweater that is like buttah, and going supercheap on a couple super "on-trend" things each year that make you feel au courant. H&M even has sustainable fashion choices now!

CK: How long does it take you to get camera-ready?

AR: My makeup routine is never more than five minutes, even if I am going red carpet. Life is too short. The extra time you spend meditating/dancing/playing with your kid/having a quickie will make you look so much more beautiful in the end.

CK: Ever had a fashion disaster?

AR: I was four months pregnant and I thought I was hiding it quite well. It was my first recurring role on a fab new TV show and first day of work. I was loving life till I walked into my dressing room and along with my clothes was a set of Spanx! I felt fat, ugly, and caught. I went home crying and wailing to my husband, "They KNOW!" But actually they had no clue I was pregnant. They just put Spanx in all the dressing rooms of all the women on this particular show. That was a reality check. We don't see ourselves the way everyone else does, so don't forget how beautiful you are, even when you want to hide in a muumuu, like I do many days.

CK: What is your secret to staying glowing and healthy?

AR: Know what foods and booze tweak your body. I am not saying don't eat them, just learn the ones that make you feel good or bad and/or make you look in my case like a blowfish. Sushi is a fave and I love it, but I skip it before a 4:30 A.M. call time for filming if I don't want to have puffy eyes. I can drink vodka with no effect, but red wine kills me. I love to go to wine tastings, or drink an amazing bottle with friends sometimes, but I have to know it will wreck me visually (my husband has been known to scream upon waking next to me). For some people it's sugar; others, gluten, dairy, whatever. I am not saying skip it; I'm just saying be honest with yourself about how it makes you feel, both physically and mentally the next day. Also learn the supplements that can tame the impact. I am a fan of B-complex and NAC.

CK: How do you stay so long and lean?

AR: I love to sweat, and I believe in movement as therapy. I box, spin, cross-train, do hot sweaty rocking yoga, hike, and love any new workout. Right now some faves are IntenSati, Rise Fitness (the new VersaClimber classes), 30/60/90, and SoulCycle. I love music and working out with friends. It's about fun. It's good for your body, soul, and even your brain.

Viva la Diva

LUANN DE LESSEPS

Luann and I met for the first time sitting next to each other on a plane flying home from L.A. I was grilling the Countess of Cool like a petite filet! The royally stylish reality star looked ab fab, so I started with her thigh-high boots and worked my way up. You would have thought I was trying to make a move on her, but I really just wanted inside scoop on all things *RHONY*. Five hours and nineteen Chardonnays later, this queen and the countess were inseparable. Not only is she a Native American/French Canadian former Italian TV star with a fab jewelry line on major home-shopping channels and rocks an Hermès scarf like no other, she's a trained geriatric nurse. Hey, that could come in handy later when we are spinsters living together with fifty cats!

CK: When did you discover the power of statement jewelry?

LD: It happened organically when I moved to Milan for modeling and wound up working on a successful game show. In that environment of being surrounded by beautiful and stylish women, I discovered costume jewelry and how it could change up my look. I could wear that dress again because I changed my necklace. I learned that statement pieces can really add mileage to your wardrobe and change your look from day to night. I like to go less blingy during the day by wearing a lot of turquoise, Indian jewelry, natural stones. There's a floating pearl necklace I designed for my Countess Collection that I call my "Wilma Flintstone" necklace. With my Gotham Collection, you can turn it up for night with black and gold, Lucite, faux diamonds, and mixed metals that are reflective. My Western Chic pieces can go day or night; it depends on what you wear with them.

CK: How can we break out of the mind-set that in jewelry, more is more?

LD: You don't want to throw the eye off in too many directions. I always say it's the statement necklace or the statement earrings. It can't be both. And always a cocktail ring. That's the beauty and the power of a statement piece—that you only need one thing to make a statement. It's easy.

CK: How do you shop for jewelry-friendly clothing, so it doesn't look too overdone?

LD: Ruffles and boat necks aren't great for jewelry. You want a simple high neckline, like a crew neck, so the jewelry is lying on a canvas of fabric, or you want a neckline that gives you a triangle of clavicle where you can lay the piece directly on your skin, whether it's a scoop neck, a button-down, or a deep V. I stay away from huge patterns and go for things that are solid or have a smaller print that still works with gold jewelry. Solid looks more expensive and luxurious. If you keep the basics simple, you can update your style with accessories to stay on-trend.

CK: No one rocks a "last layer" like you do, Lu, and that's such a European thing. Tell me how to cultivate that élan. I love that word. Like I love the word "flan."

LD: I think the last layer is important because it polishes off your look. Sometimes your last piece is a great accessory, like a cape or scarf, and it almost becomes like a piece of jewelry. Whether you drape a scarf around your neck, over one shoulder or run it down your front and throw a skinny belt around your waist to keep the scarf in place, it will change up the whole neckline, almost like a jacket lapel, and frame your face.

CK: What European fashion icon inspires you?

LD: Diane von Furstenberg. Her wrap dresses have a pattern, but they're so chic that you can accessorize easily with them. There's a reason why they are still so fresh and modern today.

Happy Holidays

from our home to yours...

FLORENCE HENDERSON

I have always adored this mullet-rocking, straight-talking TV icon who just keeps getting sassier. Florence and I met on the set of *Dancing with the Stars,* and her face was so familiar to me, I swear I was having disco-era déjà vu. Who hasn't dreamed of running away from home and living with the Bradys? Surely they wouldn't notice another towhead like me. If they could put up with Oliver, they would *love* me. But I digress. I am the biggest *Brady Bunch* fan in the world, and I couldn't believe I was meeting the woman who felt like a second mother to me. We really bonded when we both did a *Dancing with the Stars* Fan Cruise together. Now we are like family. And I'm still trying to move in with her. She has a nicer house than I do.

CK: You're a famous icon in part because of your trendsetting mullet on *The Brady Bunch.* Tell us the story behind the style.

FH: I have always created my own hairstyles. Now you may think that's a good thing or a bad thing, but it has always worked for me. I thought the mullet was a fantastic hairstyle, combining both a short look and a long look. And obviously it was copied a lot!

CK: How do you look so fabulous?

FH: Well, thank you for saying I look fabulous, Carson. I have always exercised and have always been interested in good nutrition and vitamins.

CK: What is your exercise routine?

FH: I work out three times a week with a trainer. We do a combo of Pilates, TRX, weights, and cardio.

CK: On *The Brady Bunch,* everyone would wag their finger and say, "Mom always said . . ." What wise things does Florence Henderson always say?

FH: Don't buy into the myth that you lose your sexuality as you get older. I can tell you it just gets better. Don't think that after sixty-five you should dress and behave in a more sedate manner. That is BS. Do anything that you feel like doing, as long as you don't hurt yourself or someone else. Most importantly, keep a cool head and a warm heart.

Princess

VIVICA A. FOX

Who doesn't love the feminine and ferocious Vivica A. (which I'm pretty sure stands for Awesome) Fox? Vivica and I have been friends over the years working as guests together on shows like *Who Wants to Be a Millionaire?* where we first met. We've also judged *RuPaul's Drag Race* together. You really get to know a gal when you are sitting next to her for twelve hours. (Even though those shows are cut down to twenty-eight minutes, they take about twelve hours to shoot, all told.) Whether this award-winning actress and producer is donning a sparkly Jenny Packham gown and a demure updo, a flirty halter dress with long and loose waves, or bootylicious athleisure in *Kill Bill,* this no-nonsense woman knows how to command attention.

CK: Ms. Vivica, you always look so put together. What are your fashion dos?

VF: I always do my best to wear clothes that are fitted and tailored to perfection, that accentuate my curves and complement my figure! I never force fashion or wear trends that don't work for my shape. Find colors that complement your complexion, and never be afraid to stand out. Always enter the room with a smile and your head held high!

CK: How does your hair look so damn good?

VF: The Vivica Fox Hair Collection has been such a blessing because it allows you to try different styles without killing your own hair! Also, I take good care of my hair, using Paul Mitchell Tea Tree Special Shampoo and Conditioner 'cause it's rich and stimulates hair growth. It also smells great! And I love hot oil treatments like Moroccan oil on my scalp. I use a deep olive-oil hair mask for recovery after a lot of traveling and press tours to keep my hair healthy 'n' happy.

CK: How do you pamper yourself?

VF: I totally love having microdermabrasion and an oxygen facial by my fab aesthetician Sharon Stutz every two weeks. I clean my face with Dermalogica products and use Kiehl's Rosewater Toner and Shu Uemura's Depsea Facial Mist in Rose daily.

CK: On those rare days when you're feeling less than fabulous, what do you wear to bring the positivity?

VF: If I'm feeling a little down, I make sure to tell myself that it's a new day and push the reset button! I put on bright colors like yellow or red and I love wearing bright colors on my lips. Shades like red, orange, and pink with a frosty pop gloss in the middle of the lip work great! I love lipsticks and glosses by Chanel.

KAPPA KAPPA GAMMA

KATHY NAJIMY

Kathy is one of those people that even if you haven't known her for long, it feels like you've known her all your life. If this award-winning actress and producer wasn't so warm and funny, you might hate her for being so darn amazing, from nabbing an Obie to being crowned *Ms.* magazine's Woman of the Year for her human rights activism to winning *Celebrity Poker Showdown*. You go, Sister Mary Patrick! We met working together in New York City on a project called *Celebrity Autobiography*, where celebs do a live show reading the bios of other celebs . . . usually old or dead ones like Elizabeth Taylor. We became fast friends and now see each other all the time at each other's homes. I've spent many a night at Kathy's trying to keep up with Marisa Tomei playing speed charades. Note to self: Don't ever play charades with an Oscar winner!

CK: Kathy, you are a curvalicious gal. Tell me the secrets of dressing for women who don't look like ten-year-old boys.

KN: I can only speak for myself. Oh, hell, who're we kidding? I'll speak for the world. Curvy women (i.e., *not* skinny), don't feel like you have to dress in big, boxy, square-shaped clothes. Once the fashions hit size 18 they can become either circus tenty or square-shaped, boxy, ugly prisons. Check out the form-fitting pieces or ones that represent your own personal style. If you're drawn to sexy, wear the mini. Hippie? Grab the Indian-print maxi. Sporty? Grab the jodhpurs. Wear what *you* like. Reject that your choices are only "big girl clothes" with "fun, fake, huge flowers" or "plus-size" Nancy Reagan blazers. There is more out there. Look for it; don't be afraid. Don't let fashion or magazines, billboards or your family (or me) bully you. Choose what you are drawn to. I declare a war on huge ponchos, high-necked tent dresses, and boxy "old lady" suit jackets with metal buttons!

CK: Why is it important to have a sense of humor alongside a fierce sense of style?

KN: Well, it's important to have a sense of humor for any size person, wearing any style. But a lot of people don't. Carson, you are one. So if you don't have a sense of humor, it's okay, we still like you. Most important is, don't shop with fear, thinking about all the things you can't or aren't supposed to wear. And don't Internet-shop on Ambien. Basically, keep your sense of humor and keep your dignity. Follow your heart. Choose clothes the way you would choose jewelry or a bedspread or sofa. *You*-ish.

Super Model
OF THE WORLD

RUPAUL

RuPaul Charles is one of *my* fashion icons. Who else could lay claim to the title of most famous drag queen in the universe? The multitalented, award-winning singer/songwriter, author, actor, and producer is a true chameleon. Ru can look so sharp in tailored men's suits, natty shoes, and horn-rimmed glasses one minute and moments later look just as fabulous in a fishtail sequined evening gown as the host of the mega hit show *RuPaul's Drag Race*. I've always been a fan, but became a friend as Ru asked me to help judge the last two seasons of *Drag Race*. Besides having a lot of fun, I learned a lot about fashion "herstory" from Mama Ru—from style pointers on the power of silhouette and proportion to a deeper understanding that real beauty comes from within. Ru gets "tens across the board" not only for his gender-bending fashion ferociousness but also for his ability to bring out the best in everyone he encounters.

CK: What wisdom can women everywhere learn from drag?

RP: You can paint the house all you want, but if the foundation isn't strong, your house will collapse. And that foundation is from the inside out. Most people don't care about what's underneath. Drag is all about deconstructing what's underneath the psyche and why we feel the way we do about gender and artifice. It's really making fun of all those things. The truth of the matter is we are all just spiritual beings having a human experience. As Deepak Chopra said, we're all God in drag. It's important to not take our imagery or accoutrement too seriously.

CK: Wow, Ru, that's deep! How can we all become as enlightened as you?

RP: Everybody has the potential to find that space. You have to take two steps back to truly see yourself and lose your old, limited perspective, and what usually helps is meditation. I get up early every morning to do it, and this morning I did it at 4:00 A.M. It doesn't matter how much time you spend—it could be thirty seconds or fifteen minutes—as long as you connect with the source. It centers you and balances you. It keeps your equilibrium intact. Even to walk across the room or across the street, you need equilibrium, not just physically but figuratively speaking. It's not rocket science. Meditation is not levitation!

CK: Speaking of magic tricks, drag queens are masters of proportion. Tell me about that.

RP: Everything you see in nature, in art, in mathematics has to do with proportions. If you are presenting yourself or a piece of art or a piece of furniture, it is all about balance and proportion. The human eye sees things in a certain, scientific way. And you can nudge how other people see you based on nudging proportions, just like an illusion. That's why they call drag queens illusionists. If you have a short neck, you should wear your hair high, and you shouldn't wear your hair down, and it shouldn't be too long. The proportion has to work with your body. But that's all superficial stuff about how other people see you, and that begs the question: Why does it matter how other people see you?

CK: Good question. Um, can you help me with the answer?

RP: Ask yourself, *Why do I need to look great to other people? Why does it matter how I look to other people?* The whole purpose of drag is to make fun of identity. We are thumbing our noses at the idea of the concept that you must pick and choose. Do what you want to do for you. Once you understand that, then the party begins. You feel liberated when you're not weighed down by worrying what others think, whether it's the other mothers at the PTA or the in-laws or whoever. My tenth-grade teacher said, "RuPaul, do not take life too seriously." That was the best thing I ever learned in school because it really did serve me well as I got older. Since childhood, drag has just been an extension of the way I saw the world. I always felt like an alien from another planet playing dress-up, not just in feminine clothes, but in all clothes. Even my Cub Scout uniform was a costume to me. It reminds me of my famous line that I've been saying for the past thirty years: "You're born naked and the rest is drag."

CK: I couldn't have said it better, Ru. Thanks for stealing my thunder, as usual.

#MISSION ACCOMPLISHED

Ladies, as we begin our descent back into reality, make sure your seat backs, tray tables, and confidence levels are in an upright position. Make sure your seat belt is firmly fastened and all carry-on luggage is stowed under the seat in front of you. (Your emotional baggage has been checked through to its final destination: the Bermuda Triangle.) For your safety and comfort, please remain seated with your seat belt fastened until the captain turns off the "FASHION" SEAT BELT sign. That is, unless you're wearing linen or silk and are headed somewhere fabulous after this and don't want wrinkles across your crotch.

On behalf of Carson Airlines and the entire crew, I'd like to thank you for joining us for the past eight chapters. I hope you enjoyed your journey toward becoming the absolute best version of you—from the inside out and the outside in. I look forward to seeing you again in the near future, when all of these tips, tricks, mantras, and stories have sunk in and you're ready to fly solo. Yay, you! Save a seat for me! I'll be waiting for an upgrade with a dry martini and my Evian mister!

Hard at work eating green goddess salads at the Coral
Casino beach club in Montecito, California #hateus

ACKNOWLEDGMENTS

JUST LIKE SPACE TRAVEL, OPEN-HEART surgery, and genome mapping, writing a book on style is Hard Work! Clearly, this task was grueling, as you can see from our photo. There were taxing afternoon brainstorming sessions by the pool, late nights filled with friends and truffle fries, stressful Christmas parties analyzing each other's outfits while slurping Carson's North Carolina moonshine and . . . oh wait, neither of us remembers anything after that.

But we do remember the fabulous group of people who made this book possible, so let us tip our fedoras to you, honey boos! Our amazing editors, BJ Berti and Courtney Littler, you fierce femmes of the Flatiron, we heart you! Laura Nolan and Madeleine Morel, you are the matchmakers who brought the two of us star-crossed style lovers together (we'll send pics from the honeymoon!) and got this book off to the races. Paintbrush-wizard Pepper Tharp, you truly brought our words to life with your sassy illustrations. Shubhani Sarkar, Michael Storrings, and the St. Martin's team, your vision for this book was 20/20 and we want to tattoo the cover font on our you-know-wheres! Amy Unzen, your photo-ninja skills are unmatched. Matt Albiani, legendary photographer, thank you for your decades of friendship and for not making Carson's butt look big in this book.

Special thanks go to the following talents, who contributed their expertise and star power to make this book sing like Beyoncé. Cory Bishop, Ashley Loewen, Marco Pelusi, Hector Pocasangre, you are in the style maven circle of trust. RuPaul Charles, Luann De Lesseps, Vivica A. Fox, Florence Henderson, Kym Johnson, Cyndi Lauper, Kathy Najimy, Alysia Reiner, Anansa Sims, Heather Thomson, and Ginger Zee, each of you shines like the top of the Chrysler Building. We are forever grateful for your generosity of spirit.

To Cher, Claire Danes, Ellen DeGeneres, Jane Fonda, Tom Ford, Jean Paul Gaultier, Christina Hendricks, Carolina Herrera, Mindy Kaling, Kim Kardashian, Gayle King, Ralph Lauren, Julia Louis-Dreyfus, Marsha Mason, Melissa McCarthy, Megan Mullally, Oprah, Dolly Parton, Amy Poehler, Carine Roitfeld, Amy Schumer, Gabourey Sidibe, Emma Stone, Sharon Stone, Charlize Theron, Anna Trebunskaya, Diane von Furstenberg, Serena Williams, Rachel Zoe, and the dearly departed Kevyn Aucoin, Coco Chanel, Christian Dior, Nora Ephron, Judy Garland, Edith Head, Katharine Hepburn, Joan Rivers, Elizabeth Taylor, and Gore Vidal, thank you for being the golden links on this Chanel bag.

Our superheroes Greg Clark, Jon-Claude and Grant Zucconi: We are indebted to you for putting up with us over the past year. We know that fashion people on a deadline can be cranky. Thank you for loving us anyway.

Mwah,

Carson and Riann

finis